Theme Adventures

Bright Ideas to Turn
Any Day into a Classroom Celebration

Written and illustrated by
Veronica Terrill

W9-AEE-008

Cover by Veronica Terrill

Copyright © Good Apple, 1992

ISBN No. 0-86653-610-8

Printing No. 987654

Good Apple
1204 Buchanan St., Box 299
Carthage, IL 62321-0299

SIMON & SCHUSTER *A Paramount Communications Company*

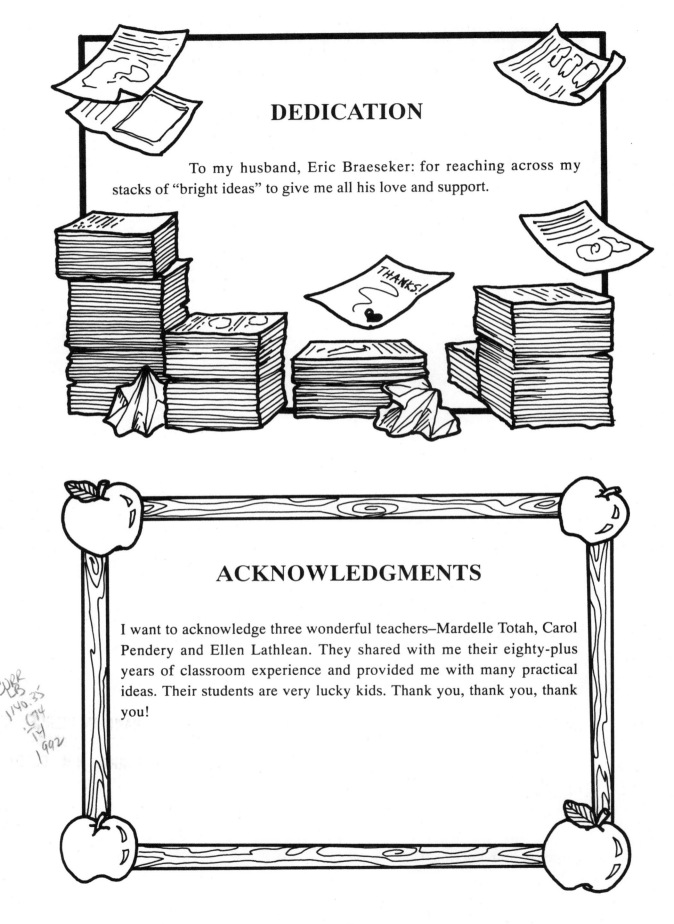

DEDICATION

To my husband, Eric Braeseker: for reaching across my stacks of "bright ideas" to give me all his love and support.

ACKNOWLEDGMENTS

I want to acknowledge three wonderful teachers–Mardelle Totah, Carol Pendery and Ellen Lathlean. They shared with me their eighty-plus years of classroom experience and provided me with many practical ideas. Their students are very lucky kids. Thank you, thank you, thank you!

GA1394

TABLE OF CONTENTS

GA1394

GA1394

INTRODUCTION

Theme Adventures is a sourcebook filled with pages of great ideas for your classroom–activities, crafts, activity pages, bulletin boards, room decorations and many other teacher "helpers." The book is divided into ten sections, with each section relating to a theme. By combining the activities and ideas in a section, you can create a special day filled with learning and fun that will delight your students. Use the themes to break out of the usual routine or coordinate with your curriculum. Try the " 'Tree'mendous Trees" section to celebrate Earth Day or Arbor Day. Use the ideas in "Make a Monster" to get your students in the mood for Halloween and create wonderfully spooky room decorations. The ideas in the "Take a Trip" section will make foreign countries come alive as students plan their trips and sample native foods. You can even use the themes in *Theme Adventures* to highlight your local events, such as planning a Smart Cookie Day around a P.T.A. bake sale. How about "All About Apples" to celebrate your town's fall harvest activities. Just use your imagination and have fun!

Each theme section contains:

Activity–Ideas for field trips, guest speakers or in-room events that provide a central activity for exploring the theme with basic information or hands-on experience

Visuals–Bulletin boards, posters or room decorations, with reproducible patterns, that will help you create colorful visual reminders of the theme

Snack Time Suggestions–Yummy ideas for theme-related foods. Some sections include patterns for straw-toppers, place mats or other ideas to add something special to your snack time.

Games and Songs–Fun and active ideas for games, with song suggestions for indoors or out

GA1394

Circle Time–Ideas for further exploration of the theme or a related subject in a quiet setting. Some Circle Times incorporate familiar children's books or stories to expand on the theme.

 Activity Page–Basic skills, such as shape recognition, math concepts and color, are reinforced in these easy-to-use reproducible sheets, which can also be used as homework pages.

 Imagination Page–A special desk activity that gives the student a chance to use his imagination to explore the theme on his own. These also provide the teacher with structured time to set up other activities.

 Crafts–Ideas and patterns for exploring the theme through art. Some finished projects may also be used as gifts.

 Take-Homes–Patterns to make awards, bookmarks, doorknob hangers and other fun projects to take home and share the theme with parents

 Extras–A potpourri of bonus ideas and projects

GA1394

In some sections you will also find convenient reproducible maps, cut-apart subject cards or learning center handouts to help put the themes together. After the theme sections, there are several pages of reproducible patterns for awards and communication sheets, as well as a handy page of theme clip art to personalize your newsletters or announcements. Each page of ideas may also be used independently, to supplement your curriculum. The activity pages and imagination pages work well as homework sheets.

Although the suggested grade level for this book is k through 2, you may want to adapt some of the ideas, taking into consideration the skill level, personality, size, etc., of your particular class. For example, the "Weather Diary" may be a great take-home activity for your first or second graders, but would be adaptable for a group classroom activity for younger students. You could enlarge the diary to poster size and fill it out in class, with students offering their observations. The "Smart Cookies" activity suggests baking cookies, but you can substitute your favorite no-bake cookie recipe. Your students will still benefit from the activity through observing the measuring and mixing.

Be sure to look around your classroom, school and community for additional resources you can utilize. Perhaps your classmate has a playhouse that would be great to use to present the "Home Sweet Home" section. Label the areas of the house, such as "window," or organize a spring cleanup. Talk to other teachers for resources like shell collections for "Under the Sea" or foreign souvenirs for "Take a Trip." Be sure to ask the parents. Some may have occupations or hobbies that they would share with your class. A bonsai tree collection would make a wonderful display for the " 'Tree'mendous Trees" section. A community theatre's costume department may be able to loan you masks and props to create a very special "Make a Monster" exhibit. You may be lucky enough to have an apple orchard nearby that will illustrate the "All About Apples" section beautifully. A simple search may yield many economical resources that are yours for the asking. Don't forget to add some of your own bright ideas!

GA1394

GENERAL INSTRUCTIONS

The pages in this book are easily duplicated for use as handouts or patterns. Here are a few helpful hints to help you prepare the pages and projects.

To reproduce as activity pages: Cover any teacher's instructions with correction fluid or white paper before you make any copies. You can also add any changes at this time, such as bookmark strips or wording.

For small designs: Reproduce just enough items to fit on a page. Trim excess paper from your items and paste close together, but not touching, on an 8 1/2" x 11" (21.57 x 27.94 cm) sheet of paper. Make your copies from this "master sheet" and you'll save time and paper.

To resize patterns: Many copy machines have enlargement/reduction capabilities that will enable you to adjust the patterns to fit your needs. Overhead or opaque projectors also work well.

To add color: You can use regular copy paper when you will be coloring the projects with crayons, chalk or pencils. For better results when using a wet medium, such as watercolors, reproduce on a heavier weight paper.

To reuse: For items you would like to use year after year, teacher's samples and pass-around cards for example, copy the item on heavier paper and laminate it after you have added any color.

To create additional decorations: You can enlarge extra copies of the bulletin board patterns or awards for use as room or door decorations. For giant 3-D decorations: Enlarge the pattern with an opaque projector, color and cut out. Trace the outline of the cutout pattern onto a sheet of lightweight paper and cut out. Staple or glue the pattern to this sheet, leaving a small opening. Stuff the pattern lightly with newspaper or tissue paper and close the opening. Tie a colorful yarn to the top and hang from the ceiling or attach to the wall.

SMART COOKIES

ACTIVITY
Field Trip/Guests

Plan a field trip to a local bakery. Don't overlook the bakery in your neighborhood supermarket. Give each child a copy of the scavenger hunt list below and have him cross off each item as he finds it. Before the trip prepare a list of questions to ask the baker, such as the time he starts to bake each morning and the number of cookies he bakes each day. Be sure to point out the comparisons between the bakery and their own kitchens. The large-size ovens and mixers would make good examples. Try to arrange for cookie samples at the end of the tour. Looking at all of the goodies will make everyone hungry.

Alternate Idea: The school cafeteria could be used for a cookie-making demonstration. Choose a simple recipe and premeasure the ingredients. Label each container and pass out copies of the recipe to each student. Have students follow along as you make the cookies.

I saw:

Name _____

What I liked best:

_____

_____

GA1394

We're Smart Cookies!

Eric · Drew · Molly · Alec · Jan · Beth · Ann · Greg · Meg · Terri · Joe · Laurie · Bill · Mack · Jared · Gene · Amanda · Mike · Andy

2" 2"

cardboard

CUT
AWAY

BULLETIN BOARD/VISUALS

Directions:

1. Using a piece of cardboard in proportion to your bulletin board, cut out two triangles, following the diagram. Cover the board with foil.

2. Cut two mitts from colorful paper (wallpaper or wrapping paper) using the pattern on page 3, flipping the pattern over to cut the opposite mitt.

3. Center the cardboard and attach the mitts and board, as shown. Letter the heading across the top.

4. Reproduce the cookie pattern on this page and give one to each student to "decorate" with crayons and write his name on it. Pin or tape the "cookies" to the "cookie sheet."

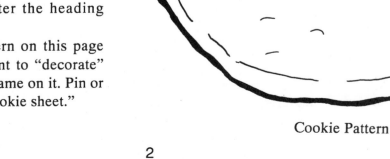

Cookie Pattern

GA1394

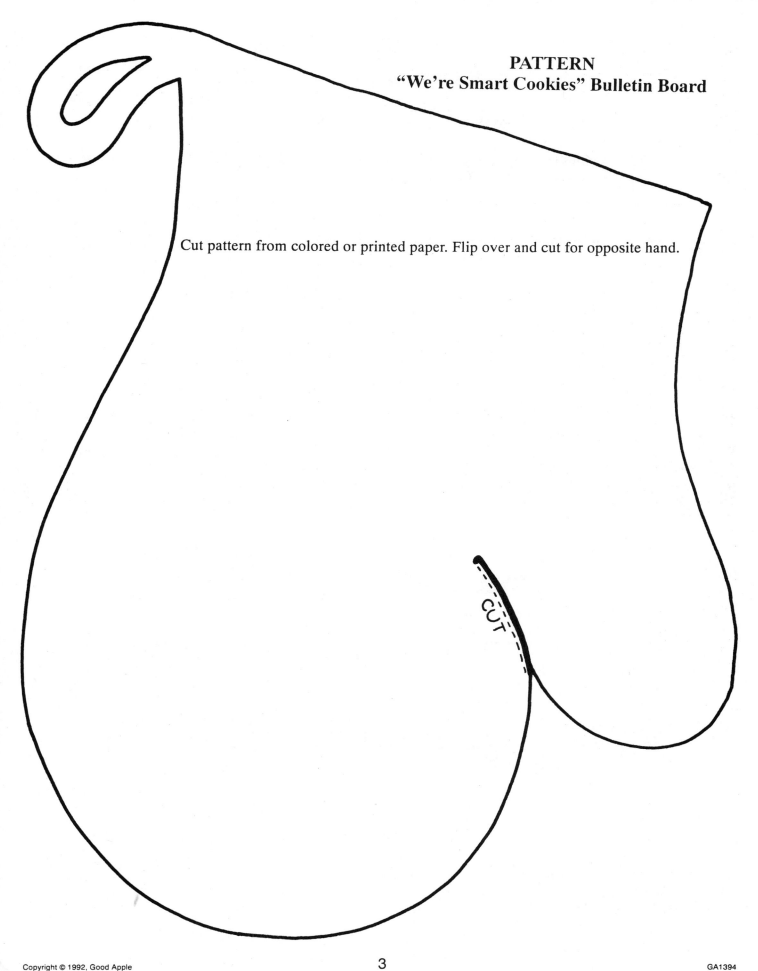

PATTERN
"We're Smart Cookies" Bulletin Board

Cut pattern from colored or printed paper. Flip over and cut for opposite hand.

CUT

3

GA1394

SNACK TIME SUGGESTIONS
Decorate your own cookie!

Materials:

    recipe cards, one per child

    plain, hard cookies (about 3" [7.62 cm] in diameter)

    cans of ready-made frosting, at room temperature

    assorted toppings, such as raisins, small chocolate chips, sprinkles, cereal, etc.

    muffin tins or small cups to organize topping

    plastic blunt-point knives and spoons

Give each child a recipe card, plastic knife, spoon and cookie. Place frosting and toppings in the center of each table. Have the children frost and decorate their cookies, following the directions on the recipe cards. (For younger children the cookies may be frosted ahead of time.) Eat and enjoy!

Additional Activity: Children could list the toppings they used or draw pictures of their cookies on the backs of their recipe cards.

Name _____

cookie   frosting   knife   toppings   spoon

1.   2.   3.   4.

GAMES AND SONGS
Hot Cookie

The rules for this game are the same as Hot Potato, except you substitute a "cookie" (see below) for the potato. The children sit in a circle and pass the "hot cookie" until the music stops. Whoever is holding the cookie is out. The game continues until only one child remains. Use music with a cookie theme, such as *Sesame Street*'s "C Is for Cookie."

cardboard "cookie" with Styrofoam filling and paper icing

flour and Salt dough "cookie"

wrapped real cookie

plastic cookie cutter

GA1394

ACTIVITY PAGE
Cookie Shape Search

1. Draw a line under the square cookie.
2. Put an X on the round cookies.
3. Draw circles around the triangle-shaped cookies.
4. Color the rectangle-shaped cookies brown.

6

GA1394

CIRCLE TIME
Class Cookie Batter

Reproduce and cut apart sets of the ingredient cards below. Pass one card out to each student and explain that it takes many ingredients to make a cookie and that each one is important. Have the children gather in groups, by matching their cards. Tell the children that you are going to be mixing up a batch of cookies and as you call out each ingredient, that group must come into the mixing bowl (rug) and sit quietly until you've added all the rest of the ingredients. Pretend to stir the "dough" and explain that in order to "bake," all the ingredients must be very still. Now it's time to read your favorite cookie story, such as "The Little Gingerbread Boy." As an additional activity, you can set up a display of various sizes of measuring cups and spoons. Provide large bowls of uncooked rice, and let the children experiment with measuring the rice and comparing the differences between the cups and spoons.

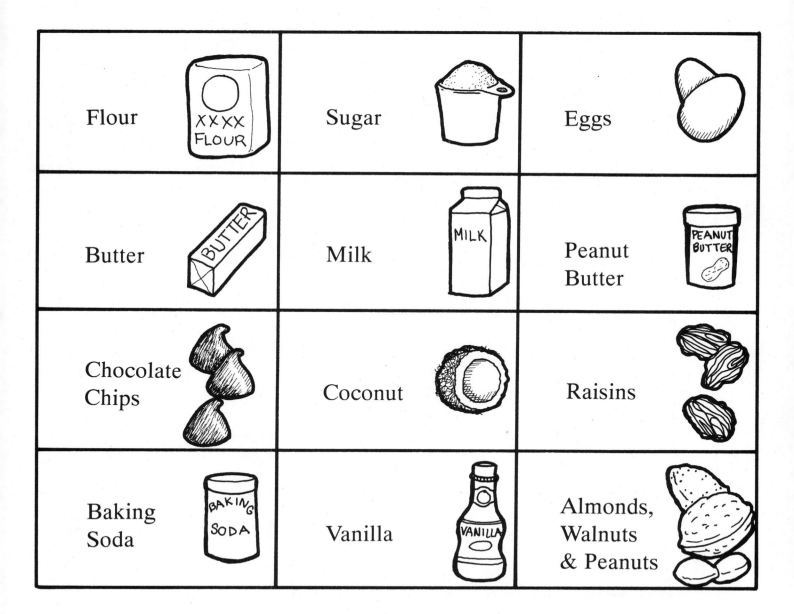

GA1394

IMAGINATION PAGE

Imagine you are a cookie. What kind would you be? Draw a picture of what you would look like.

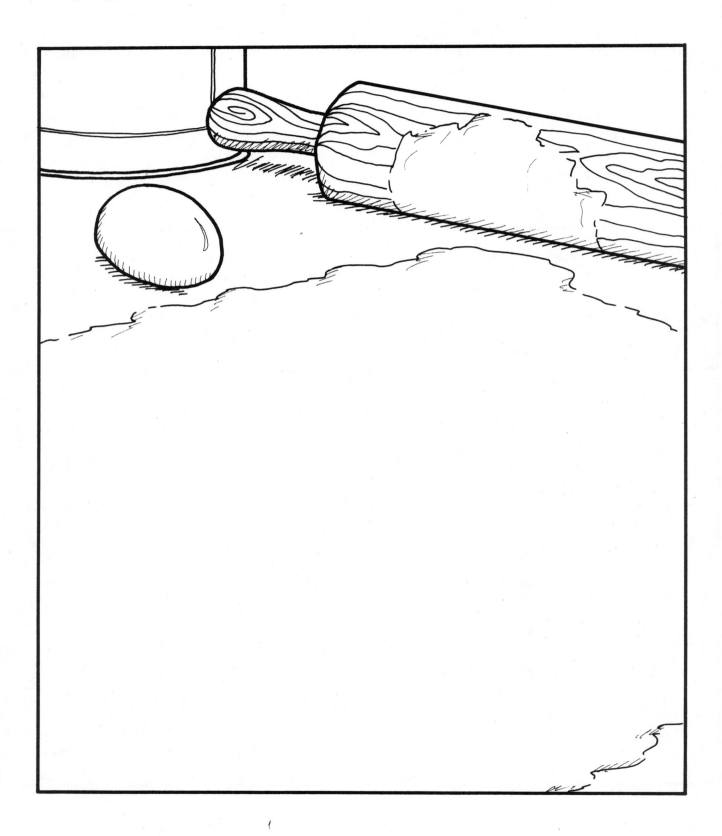

GA1394

CRAFTS
Design a Cookie

Reproduce the gingerbread cookie pattern on dark-tan or brown paper. Have the children cut them out and "decorate" their cookies using crayons or chalk. Glitter, rickrack and buttons may also be used to design the cookies. Try stringing these together for cute room decorations at Christmas.

GA1394

TAKE-HOMES
Cookie Badge

Reproduce badge on heavy paper. Cut out and put child's name in the box. Fold tab on dotted line and tuck in child's neckline or cut off tab and pin badge on.

I'm a smart cookie!

10

GA1394

EXTRAS
Cookie Baker's Hat

Reproduce the patterns below on heavy white paper. Cut out on the heavy lines and attach the two straight strips to the main hat with tape or staples. Size to fit each child's head and wear while doing the snack time activity.

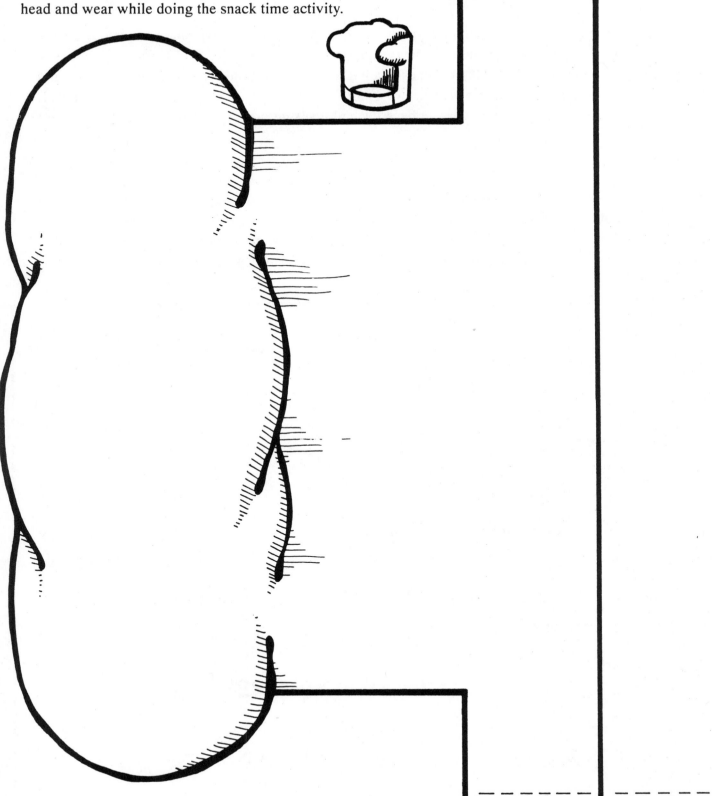

11

GA1394

UNDER THE SEA

ACTIVITY
Guest–Our New Fish

Add a new fish or two to your classroom aquarium. If your room doesn't have one, you may be able to purchase or borrow one. Have a contest to name the newcomer(s). Give each child an entry blank below or take the entries verbally. Place all the names in a bag and draw the fish's new name. Have each child draw a picture of the fish and write a sentence or a story about the newcomer. You could design a welcome banner to hang over the aquarium and have the children sign their names and perhaps write short welcome messages.

Field Trip

Arrange to visit an aquarium or fish/pet store. Prepare for the trip by reading stories and science books about fish and life under the water. Tell each child to pick out his favorite fish and remember its color, or for older children, what it looks like. When you get back to class, graph the favorite colors or have older children draw or paint pictures of their favorite fish. If you are unable to arrange a field trip, you could show a travel or science film and follow the same activities.

GA1394

BULLETIN BOARD/VISUALS

Directions:

1. Cover the top two-thirds of the bulletin board with blue paper and the bottom third with tan. (You can also use sandpaper to create a "sandy" ocean floor.)

2. Reproduce the patterns on pages 14 and 15, adjusting the sizes if needed to fit your board. Color and cut out. Attach them to the board.

3. Cut out the title "bubble" and letter the title as illustrated. Attach to the board.

4. If you would like, stretch plastic wrap or cellophane across the board in rows and staple the ends, as illustrated, to give the board an "underwater" look.

GA1394

PATTERNS

14

GA1394

SNACK TIME SUGGESTIONS

Fish Crackers

Goldfish-shaped crackers and small broccoli spears. Serve these on blue napkins or plates.

Jell-O Fishbowl

Green Jell-O with green or purple grapes added, before the Jell-O has set. Serve this in a clear plastic cup, if possible, so the children can see the "fish."

Seafoam Punch

Lemon-lime pop with lime sherbet added. Serve in a cup with a straw and the starfish cup decoration.

Reproduce, cut out and glue or tape to the side of a cup, as shown.

Pattern

16

GA1394

GAMES AND SONGS
Fishing for Fun

Reproduce and cut out the fish pattern below. On each fish write an activity, such as "Hop on one foot three times," "Do four jumping jacks" or "Run to the slide and slide down." Put a paper clip on each fish, as shown. Tie a string to a magnet and then to a yardstick or pointer. Place all the fish in a large shallow box or scatter them in a corner of the room. Give each child a chance to be the "fisherman," and follow the directions on his catch. Play background music from Disney's *The Little Mermaid* movie soundtrack.

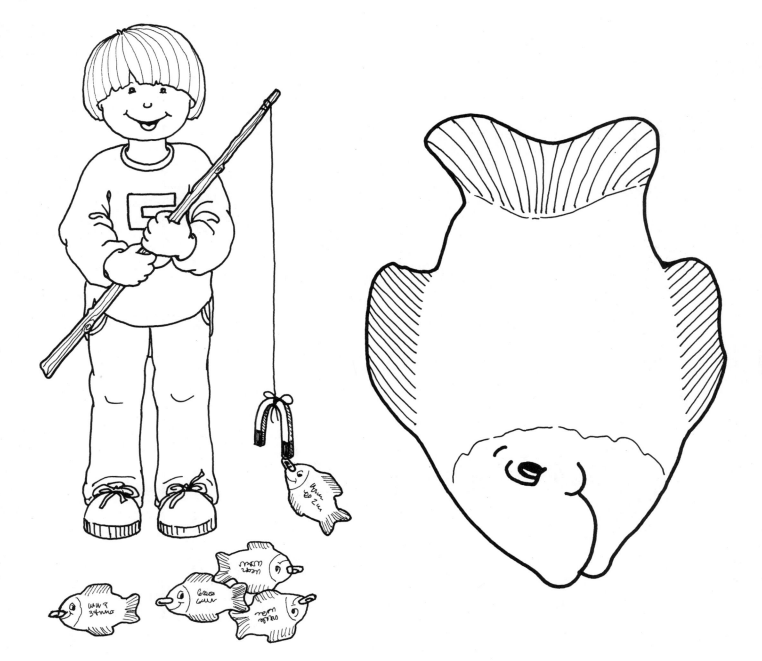

GA1394

ACTIVITY PAGE
Under the Sea Search

Look in the big picture for the "sea" things shown in the little boxes. Count each one and write the number in the box. Color the picture.

How many?

How many?

How many?

How many?

GA1394

CIRCLE TIME
Seashells by the Seashore

Use this time to explore some of the wonderful natural treasures found in our oceans. Copy, cut out and laminate the seashell cards below. Pass the cards around and discuss how the shells were once homes for sea creatures. If you have access to a shell collection, find shells that resemble the shells pictured on the cards. Bury the shells in a dishpan of sand. Have the children reach in the sand, pick out a shell and match it to a card. Pass around a conch shell and let the children hear the ocean roar inside. Discuss how important the oceans are to our planet and the environmental concerns we have about them. Ask the children for ideas about protecting our oceans and share with them the things they can do, such as not releasing helium balloons and cutting apart plastic six-pack rings before they throw them out. Play a recording of the sounds of the ocean while the children close their eyes and pretend they are at the seashore.

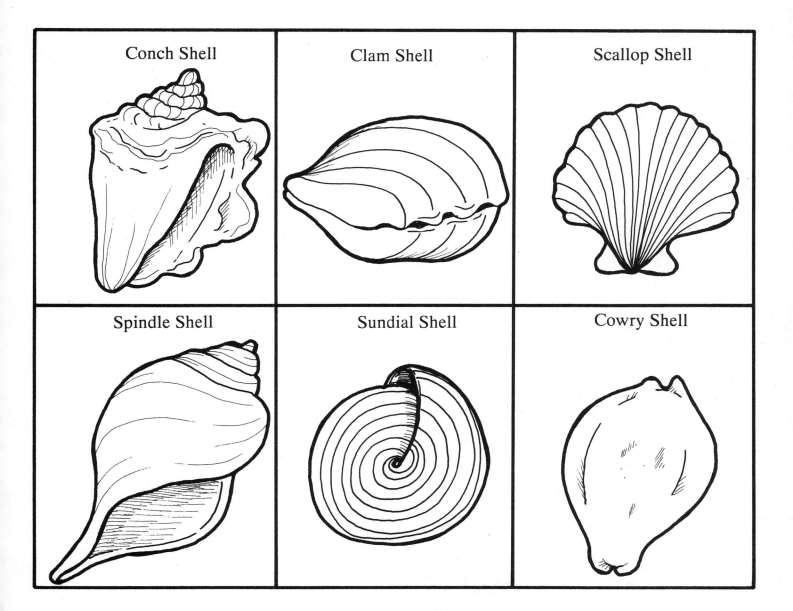

| Conch Shell | Clam Shell | Scallop Shell |
| Spindle Shell | Sundial Shell | Cowry Shell |

GA1394

IMAGINATION PAGE

Imagine you are a scuba diver deep under the sea. You've just discovered a new fish, never before seen. Draw a picture of it here.

GA1394

CRAFTS
Undersea Mobile

From heavy blue paper cut two "wave" toppers from the pattern below. Cut out the sea creatures from colored paper. Punch out the holes and assemble, with string, as shown.

CUT TWO

GA1394

TAKE-HOMES
Octopus Finger Puppet

Reproduce the pattern below on heavy paper. Color and cut out. Also cut out the two circles for fingers. Insert index and third fingers in the holes and use for stories, plays and "dancing" along to music.

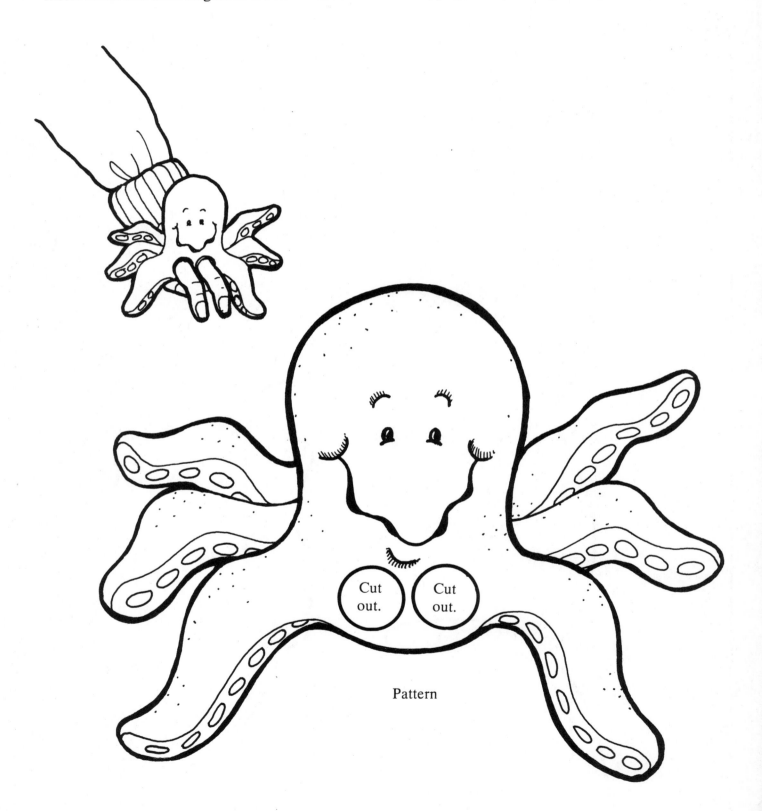

Cut out.

Cut out.

Pattern

22

EXTRAS
Under the Sea Shadow Box

Reduce the illustrations on pages 14 and 15. Color, cut out and paste the figures to tabs as shown below. You may wish to leave a few without tabs, to paste on the back wall or floor of the box. Paint or color the inside of a shoe box bottom blue. Paste the tabs to the bottom or sides of the shadow box, as illustrated. You can leave the bottom of the box as is, or sprinkle the base with sand and small shells and stones.

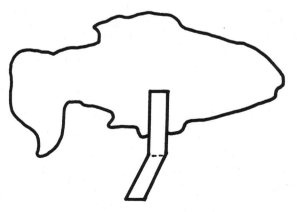

TEDDY BEAR BUDDIES

ACTIVITY
Teddy Bear Hunt

Make copies of the teddy bear pattern below, using light-brown or tan paper, if possible. Laminate them if you wish. Now decide on a location for your hunt. Here are some possibilities.

Your Classroom: Hide the bears around the classroom. Place them in activity books, among plants, peeking out from behind papers on the bulletin board. Children will be delighted to find bears hiding in their backpacks or cubbyholes. You may wish to place a limit on the number of bears per child and have them return to their seats for the next activity when they reach it. Don't forget to hide enough bears so every child will be a successful hunter. You can whisper hints to help the ones that need it.

The Library: The teddy bears can be hidden randomly peeking out of books and magazines. Be sure to bend their paws over the pages as illustrated below, or your bears may be in hiding quite a while! For a more complex project, make a list of books (including catalog numbers) and hide a bear in each one. Have each child search for a book and find the bear hidden inside. On the back of the found bear, have each child write the title, author and one other fact about the book such as category or publisher.

Additional Activity: Place a gold star or sticker on some of the bears. Award special prizes, bookmarks and badges, for example, to the lucky hunters.

BULLETIN BOARD/VISUALS

Directions:

1. Cover the bulletin board with light-blue paper.
2. On tan-colored paper, reproduce two paw patterns on this page and the head and foot pattern on page 26, for each paper you want to display.
3. Attach the papers and pattern parts as shown.
4. Letter the heading at the top of the board.
5. Glue large foil stars on the blue background to decorate the space between the bears.

Rotate the best papers, until all of your students have been able to display their "beary" best work.

Paw Pattern

GA1394

PATTERNS

Head Pattern

Foot Pattern

26

SNACK TIME SUGGESTIONS

Teddy bear-shaped crackers or cookies. These can be served as is or "glued" with frosting to a graham cracker.

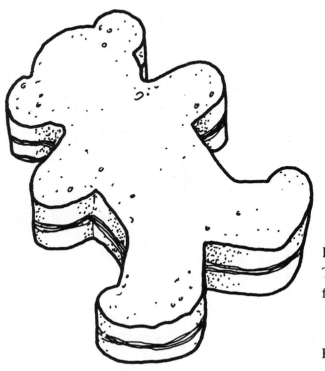

Peanut butter and honey on whole wheat bread. To make it extra special, cut out a bear shape from the sandwich, using a cookie cutter.

Honey and butter on biscuits.

Below is a pattern for a napkin ring. Reproduce the pattern on colorful paper and cut out. Glue where shown and insert rolled napkin into the ring.

GA1394

GAMES AND SONGS
Feed the Bear Beanbag Toss

Enlarge the pattern below onto heavy cardboard and cut out, including the bear's mouth, as illustrated. Position the bear head on the side of a medium-sized cardboard box and trace the shape of the mouth opening onto the side of the box. Remove the bear's head and cut out the traced area on the side of the box. Glue the bear head on the side of the box, matching the openings. Have the children line up in front of the box (determine the distance away from the box based on skill level). The children then take turns throwing beanbags or balls into the bear's mouth, trying to feed him. To make the game competitive, give each child a turn. When a child misses, he is out. Continue taking turns, taking a small step back each turn, until only one child is left.

Cut out.

Pattern

GA1394

	Brown		Red
	Yellow		Blue
	Pink		Green

GA1394

CIRCLE TIME
"Goldilocks and the Three Bears"

Following the directions on page 32, make Papa Bear, Mama Bear and Baby Bear stick puppets, and make the "Goldilocks" puppet below. Give one puppet to each child. Read the story "Goldilocks and the Three Bears." As you read the story, have the children hold up their stick puppets whenever you mention their characters. Follow the story with a discussion of the contrasts found throughout the story: hot, cold, just right, etc. Have the children give examples of each concept.

Goldilocks Stick Puppet

Reproduce the pattern on white or cream-colored paper. Assemble the puppet following the directions on page 32.

30

GA1394

IMAGINATION PAGE

Imagine it's your teddy bear's birthday. What present will you give him? Draw a picture of it in the box below.

GA1394

CRAFTS
Teddy Bear Buddy Stick Puppet

Reproduce the pattern on heavy, tan or light-brown paper. Cut out and attach the arms and legs with paper fasteners, as illustrated. Glue a craft stick to the back of the pattern to complete the puppet.

To Make the Three Bears: Follow the directions above EXCEPT vary the size that you reproduce the patterns by adjusting the copy machine as follows: Papa Bear—100% or same size, Mama Bear—85% reduction, Baby Bear—70% reduction. Color, cut out and assemble as described above.

GA1394

TAKE-HOMES
I Had a "Beary" Nice Day! Badge and Bookmark

For a Badge: Reproduce the bear pattern below on white or colored stock. Add color if you like. Cut out and safety pin or tape to student's clothes or attach to take-home papers.

For a Bookmark: Attach a 2" x 6" (5.08 x 15.24 cm) piece of colorful paper to the back of each bear pattern as shown. The bookmark strip may also be drawn on the original bear pattern before you reproduce it and cut out as one piece.

33

GA1394

EXTRAS
Teddy Bear's Den

Reproduce the bear on page 24 and the bear's house and accessories below. Let the children color and cut everything out and design their own houses, adding their own ideas, such as pictures and furniture. When they decide on a favorite arrangement, have them paste everything in place to save and display all the great designs.

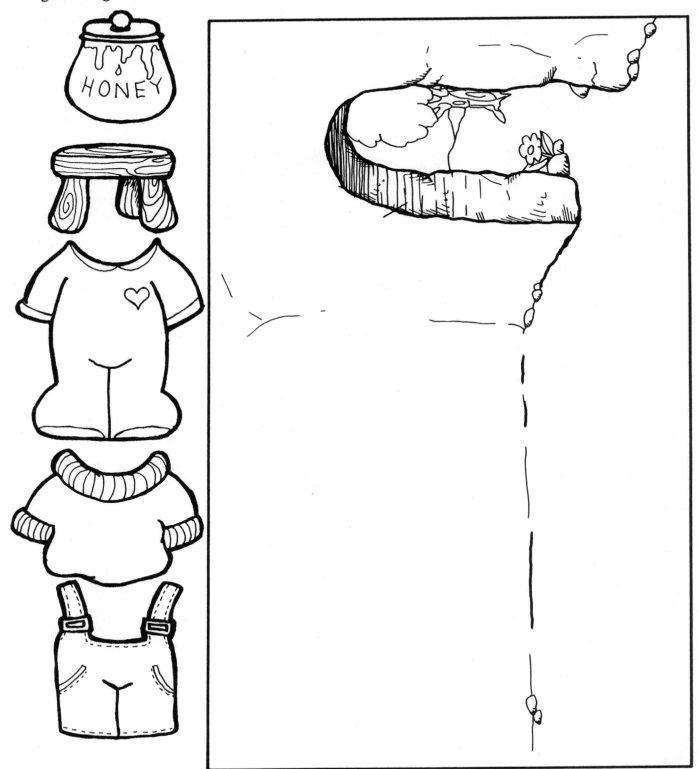

34

WEATHER WATCHERS

ACTIVITY
Videotape Exploration

"How to watch our weather." Prepare a videotape of your local weather report. (You may need permission from the TV station to do this.) Play the tape for your class the next day. Pause the tape frequently and discuss the segments presented in the report. Discuss the national and local maps. Children can name the cities or states that their relatives live in and can explain the weather report for those areas. Point out the symbols on the maps and explain them, as well as the high and low temperatures. Be sure to explain any unusual weather, such as tornadoes or hurricanes. Discuss the forecasting segment and compare it to the actual weather. How close did they come to predicting it? Explain to the children that the weather reports they see on TV or read in the paper are the final step in a long process of weather forecasting and that many people are involved in bringing the weather reports to the public. For older grades, you can discuss the jobs, such as meteorologists, and the training they must have to watch the weather. Give the children copies of the weather diary on page 46, and have them watch the local weather for a week. They can make a pair of Weather Watcher Binoculars, illustrated below, to help them watch.

Weather Watcher Binoculars

Cover or paint two cardboard tubes from toilet paper or paper towels. Place the rolls next to each other, as illustrated, and secure with rubber bands.

Note: You can substitute tubes made from rolled heavy paper, if the cardboard tubes are not available.

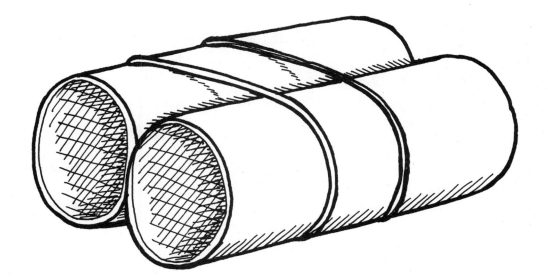

GA1394

BULLETIN BOARD/VISUALS

Directions:

1. Cover the bulletin board with blue paper.
2. Reproduce the patterns on pages 37 and 38, adjusting the sizes if needed to fit your board. Color and cut out. Attach them to the board, as shown.
3. Letter the title at the top of the board.
4. Cut out a long rectangle from heavy yellow or white paper. Cut one end into an arrow shape. Attach to the board with a thumbtack or pushpin, so it can swing from side to side.
5. Pick a time of the day to have a child position the arrow to show the weather.

Note: The weather symbol patterns can be reduced and glued to the tops of papers as story starters. The stories can be displayed on the board if you have extra room.

PATTERNS

GA1394

GA1394

My Weather Book

Reproduce the book below. Fold in half and in half again to create a book.

My Weather Book

Name _____

the sun

Every type of weather is made by the sun. The sun warms our Earth and the air above it. Wind is caused by cool air moving toward warm or warm air moving toward cool.

clouds

Clouds are made of tiny droplets of water vapor that clump together as they rise from the earth and cool. (When it's very cold, clouds have tiny specks of ice in them, too.)

rain

When the water droplets in clouds get too heavy to float in the air, they fall to Earth as rain.

thunder and lightning

BOOM!

Lightning is a giant electric spark. Thunder is the sound the air makes when lightning pushes it fast and hard.

snow

Snow is made when the water in the clouds freeze into crystals and fall to the ground.

rainbow

A rainbow is made when the light from the sun is bent and spread apart when it shines through falling raindrops.

GA1394

SNACK TIME SUGGESTIONS

Snowballs

Using your favorite recipe, make small-sized popcorn balls. Serve with icy-cold juice.

Catch a Cloud

Place a dab of marshmallow creme between two graham cracker squares.

Slushes

In a blender, mix together juice with several ice cubes, until the ice is finely crushed. Serve in a cup with a straw decorated with the Storm Cloud Straw Topper below.

Storm Cloud Straw Topper

Reproduce the pattern. Cut out and punch out the holes. Push a drinking straw through, as illustrated above, to decorate the straws.

GA1394

GAMES AND SONGS
Freeze and Thaw

While playing a record, have the children dance around the room. The children must freeze when you stop the music and stay "frozen" in the same position until you "thaw" them (start the music). Repeat until the song is finished.

How many words can you make from the letters in the word

WEATHER?

Write them on the lines below.

_____   _____

_____   _____

_____   _____

_____   _____

_____   _____

_____   _____

_____   _____

GA1394

CIRCLE TIME
Weather and Me

Reproduce the cards below on heavy paper. Cut apart and staple the cards to craft sticks, as shown. Put the cards in a paper bag or covered box. Pass the bag or box from one child to another. Have each pick out a stick and answer a question about how the type of weather on his stick affects one of the following:

The house you live in
The clothes you wear
Your transportation
Your recreational activities
The work people do
The food that you eat

Gear the questions to the grade level of your class, from easy (what clothes do you wear when it rains?) to more complex (what happens to the wheat crop if it doesn't rain? how will it affect the bread you buy?). Ask the children to give personal examples, such as "Have you ever had to change your plans because of rain or snow?"

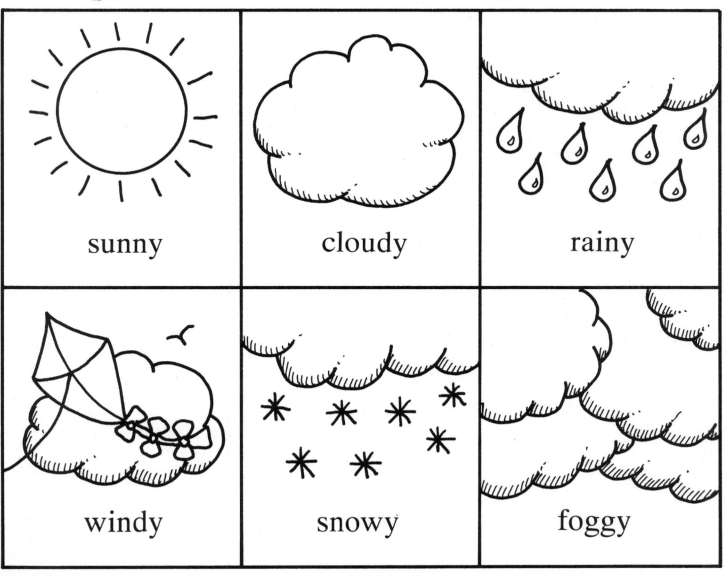

sunny

cloudy

rainy

windy

snowy

foggy

IMAGINATION PAGE

Imagine you can create a wacky rainstorm. Pretend to put two different things into the cloud below. What are they? Draw a picture of the wacky rain that would come out.

44

GA1394

CRAFTS
Sunshine Pop-up

Reproduce designs on heavy paper. Cut out, color and assemble, as shown. Glue spots of silver glitter to the cloud for a "sparkle-ly" project.

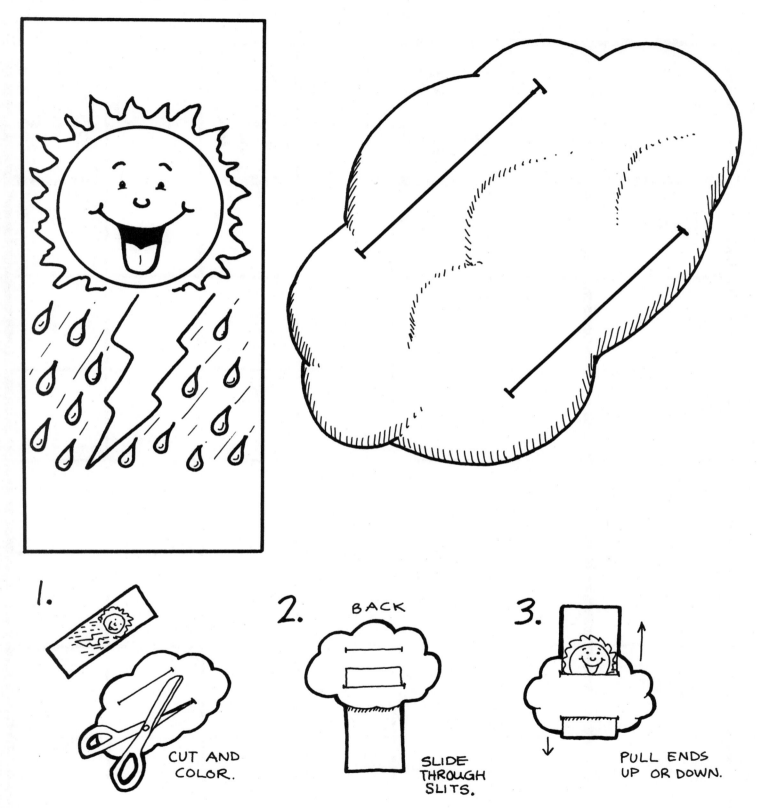

1. CUT AND COLOR.

2. BACK
SLIDE THROUGH SLITS.

3. PULL ENDS UP OR DOWN.

GA1394

TAKE-HOMES
My Weather Diary

Pick a time to check the weather each day. Put an *X* under the type of weather you see.	☀	⛅	☁	🌧	🌨	🪁
MONDAY						
TUESDAY						
WEDNESDAY						
THURSDAY						
FRIDAY						
SATURDAY						
SUNDAY						

EXTRAS
My Weather Report Card

Reproduce the pattern below on heavy paper. Cut out the circle and card, including the small window. Attach the circle to the card with a paper fastener, as illustrated. Turn the circle to report the weather.

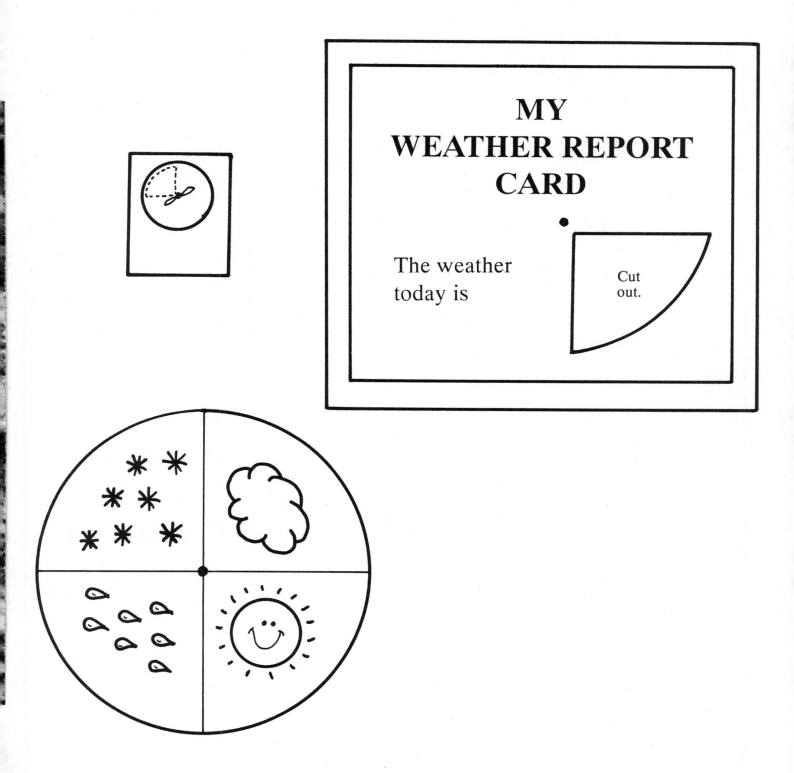

MY WEATHER REPORT CARD

The weather today is

Cut out.

GA1394

TERRIFIC TEETH

ACTIVITY
Guest

Invite a local dentist to speak to your class about tooth structure and how to take care of teeth. Many dentists can even provide visual aids, such as models or posters. Pass out copies of the card below and enlarge it to create a backdrop for the presentation. If possible, pass out new toothbrushes as a great take-home treat for tooth care "homework."

Learning Center

Create a Terrific Teeth learning center. Enlarge the cards below to make two sections of the center. Add a third panel, with a pocket, to hold the copies of "Tooth Maze" on page 53. Additional panels may be added as desired. Some ideas include

- an illustrated step-by-step lesson on proper brushing and flossing
- Attach samples of real toothbrushes, floss, etc., to a panel.
- Make a collage from magazine pictures of foods that are good for your teeth.
- pictures of healthy smiles

Note: Instructions for making a learning center can be found on page 60.

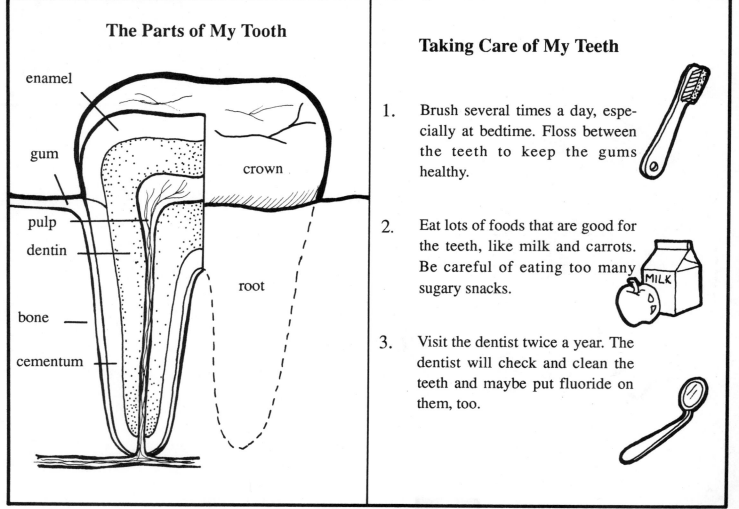

The Parts of My Tooth

enamel
gum
pulp
dentin
bone
cementum
crown
root

Taking Care of My Teeth

1. Brush several times a day, especially at bedtime. Floss between the teeth to keep the gums healthy.

2. Eat lots of foods that are good for the teeth, like milk and carrots. Be careful of eating too many sugary snacks.

3. Visit the dentist twice a year. The dentist will check and clean the teeth and maybe put fluoride on them, too.

GA1394

VISUALS
Tooth Care Cutouts

Use these cutouts to decorate posters, bulletin boards, etc. Reduce the size to paste on activity pages or use as story starters.

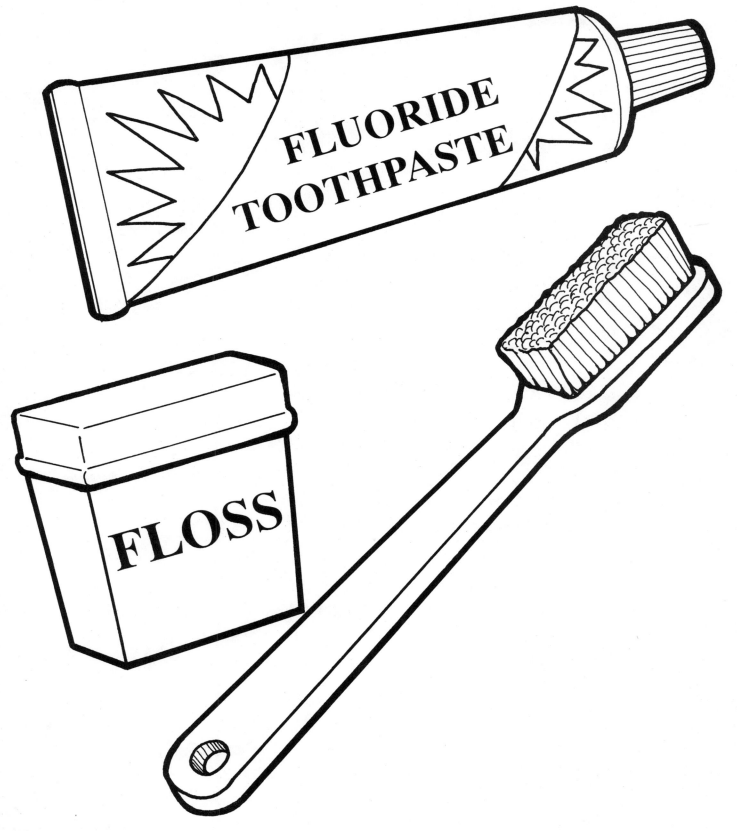

GA1394

GA1394

SNACK TIME SUGGESTIONS

Shredded Apple and Carrot Salad
Stir a little bit of lemon juice into the shredded apples to keep them from turning brown.

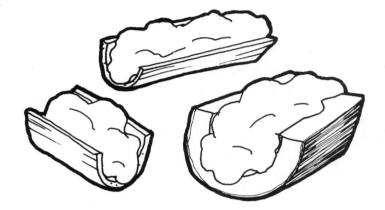

Stuffed Celery and Cucumbers
Cut cucumbers in half; scrape out seeds. Spread soft cheese in hollows of the celery and cucumber sections. Chill. Cut into small pieces.

Yogurt Add-ins
Set up several bowls of fruit, cut into small pieces. Give each child a cup of vanilla yogurt, leaving enough room in the cup for the children to stir in their own fruit.

Straw Flag Pattern
Reproduce and cut out the flag pattern below. Fold around a straw, about 1" (2.54 cm) from the top, and glue the ends together as illustrated.

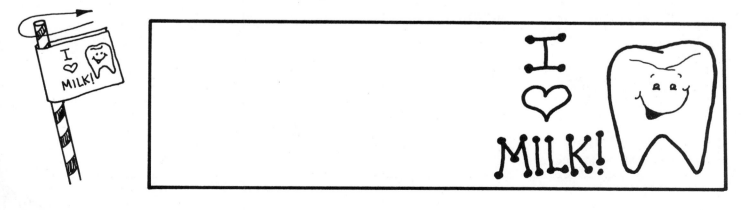

GA1394

GAMES AND SONGS
Happy Tooth Song
Sung to the tune of "Here We Go 'Round the Mulberry Bush"

Lyrics	Motions
This is the way we brush our teeth, brush our teeth, brush our teeth. This is the way we brush our teeth, so early in the morning.	(Make tooth-brushing motions with hand.)
This is the way we floss our teeth, floss our teeth, floss our teeth. This is the way we floss our teeth, to keep our gums healthy.	(Make flossing motion with hand.)
This is the way we eat healthy snacks, eat healthy snacks, eat healthy snacks. This is the way we eat healthy snacks, instead of sugary treats.	(Pretend to eat carrots and drink milk.)
This is the way we visit the dentist, visit the dentist, visit the dentist. This is the way we visit the dentist, to keep our happy smiles.	(March in place and swing arms, happily.)
This is the way we brush our teeth, brush our teeth, brush our teeth. This is the way we brush our teeth, before we go to sleep.	(Make tooth-brushing motions with hand and then tilt head to the side and pretend to sleep.)

GA1394

ACTIVITY PAGE
Tooth Maze

Help the tooth find its way to the healthy smile. Don't cross anything that might be bad for your teeth!

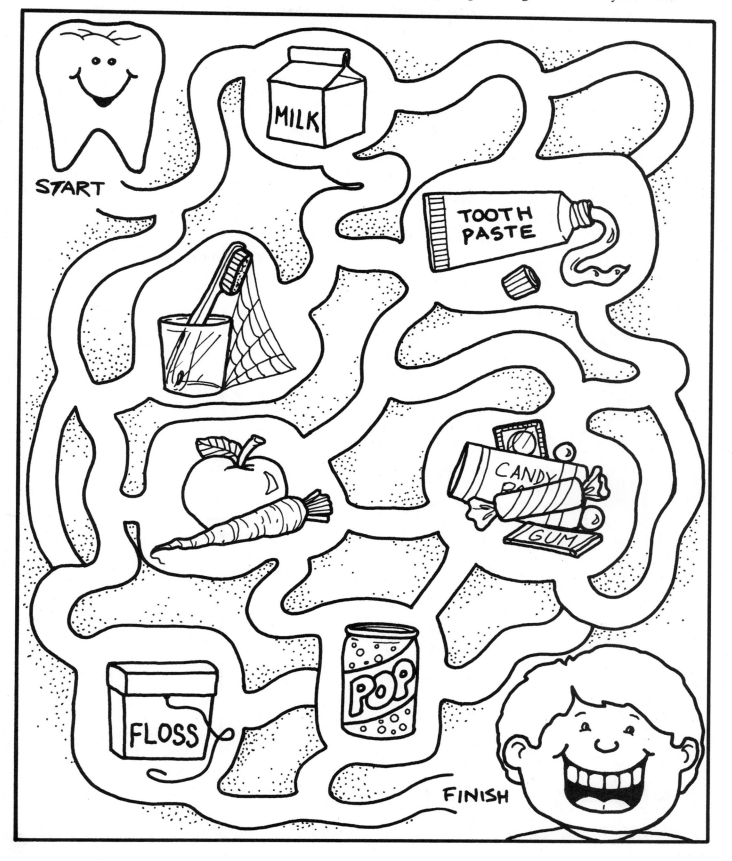

GA1394

CIRCLE TIME
More Terrific Teeth

Reproduce the card below. Cut out and fold in half on the dotted line. Glue or staple the folded card to a craft stick, as illustrated. Make a list of situations involving tooth health or safety, gearing it to the grade level of the class. As you read the situations, have the children hold up either the happy or sad tooth, depending on whether the situation is good or bad for their teeth. Situations could include chewing on a pencil, eating a carrot or drinking milk, not brushing at bedtime, throwing rocks.

Other Tooth Topics
Talking with Teeth

Have children say the word *tooth* and notice that their tongue is stopped by their teeth, to make the *T* sound. Say the other letters of the alphabet and see what other letters need "tooth helpers."

Types of Teeth

Define *incisors, canines, pre-molars* and *molars* and discuss the function of each type of tooth. Have the children try to chew a food, such as a cracker, using only their front teeth.

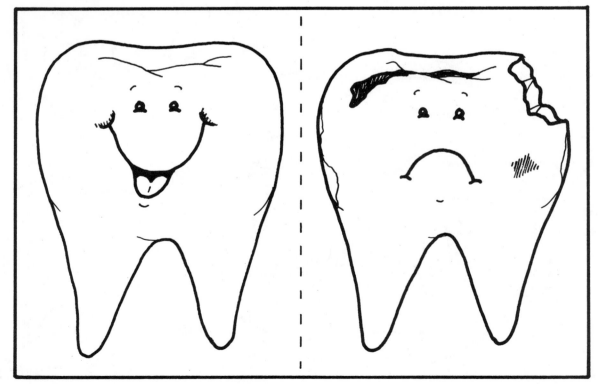

GA1394

IMAGINATION PAGE

Imagine that you have followed the Tooth Fairy home. What does she do with the teeth she collects? Draw a picture of it below.

GA1394

CRAFTS
My Tooth Pocket

This pocket can be made to store teeth lost at school or sent home for visits from the Tooth Fairy. Reproduce the pattern on white or colored paper; cut out. Following the illustrations below, fold and paste the pocket together. If used at school to store a lost tooth, place the tooth in the pocket, fold over and glue the flap or seal with a sticker. For a take-home project, make as directed above, except don't seal. This pocket can also be made out of colored felt and glued with fabric glue. Decorate the front with a tooth cut from white felt. Use the tooth shape as a pattern. Glue to the pocket with fabric glue. Cut two small slits in the flap, as shown below, and thread a piece of colorful thread through the slits; tie the pocket shut.

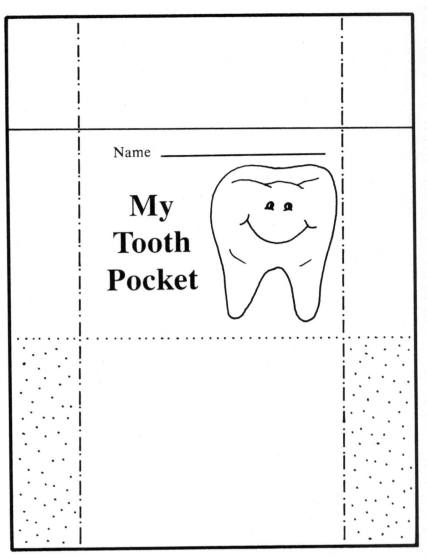

Name _____

My Tooth Pocket

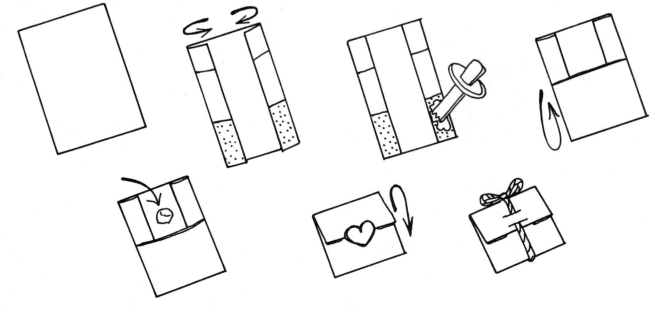

Reproduce the sign below and send it home with your students. You could also cut apart the sign on the dotted line and laminate the reminder note for a more permanent take-home project.

58

GA1394

"TREE"MENDOUS TREES

ACTIVITY
Which-Tree-Is-Which Walk

Take a walk around your school grounds or local park with a tree identification book. Keep a list of the different trees that you are able to identify. Do a bark rubbing with crayons and paper of each tree and label the rubbing. Take a leaf sample or draw a picture of a leaf from each tree. Collect any seeds or nuts and draw pictures of flowers found on the trees that you identify.

Note: The "Take-a-Trip Suitcase" project on page 115 could be made and carried on your walk to hold the samples.

During the Walk

Point out that trees keep our air clean by absorbing carbon dioxide. This gas is produced when people and animals breathe out and coal or oil is burned. The more trees that we have on our planet, the healthier our air will be.

If it's a sunny day, have the children stand in the sun and then stand in the shade of the tree. Discuss how much cooler it is in the shade and how trees also shade our homes and save energy (less air-conditioning is needed).

Trees also provide homes for birds, animals, insects *and* people. See if anyone can spot a bird's nest or other home in the trees. Talk about the lumber that makes up houses and even some schools. Discuss the importance of replanting the trees we cut down and conserving and recycling tree products.

Back in the classroom, make posters of the trees that the children have learned about. Older children can write extra facts about the trees that they look up in the tree identification book. These can be written on the posters, along with the pictures and bark rubbings. Attach the seeds or nuts to the poster and display. For additional information, write to the National Arbor Day Foundation, Arbor Lodge 100, Nebraska City, NE 68410.

GA1394

VISUALS
"Tree"mendous Trees Learning Center

This learning center will give children a chance to explore more facts about trees. Instructions are given for a four-panel (9" x 12" [22.86 x 30.48 cm] panels) center, but you can change the size or add your own panels as desired. The finished panels can be pinned to the bulletin board or attached to the sides of a box. You can also lay them flat on a table or tape the panels together accordion-style as illustrated below.

For each panel, you will need a 9" x 12" (22.86 x 30.48 cm) sheet of stiff cardboard or foam board, available at art supply stores. Cover or paint the board, if desired.

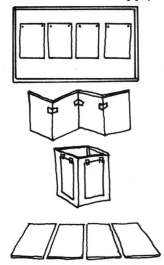

Panel 1: Attach the "Tree"mendous Trees title (page 61) to the top of the panel. Attach photos of trees and their information to fill the rest of the panel.

Panel 2: Reproduce and color the sheet on page 62 and attach to the panel.

Panel 3: Tape or staple a 9" x 6" (22.86 x 15.24 cm) sheet of heavy paper to the bottom of the panel as illustrated. Attach the "Take One" sign on page 61. Reproduce the activity on page 65 or the take-home sheet on page 69 and put in the pocket.

Panel 4: Attach the "Look!" sign on page 61 to the top of the panel and attach leaf, nut or seed samples to the rest of the panel.

If you set up your center on a table, you can also display samples of bark, tree sections, fruits or twigs with the center. Let the children visit the center in small groups to read the panels and do the activities.

GA1394

"Tree"mendous Trees!

PATTERNS
Learning Center Titles

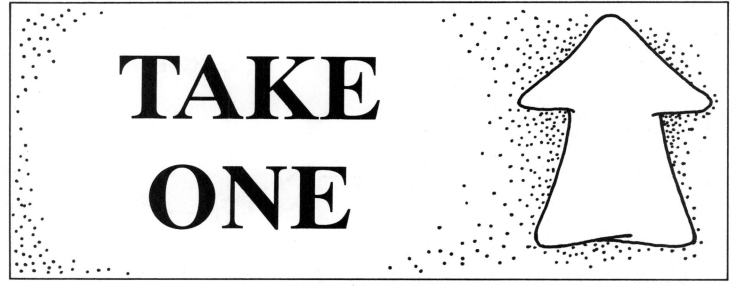

TAKE ONE

LOOK! HAVE YOU SEEN THESE ON TREES?

61

GA1394

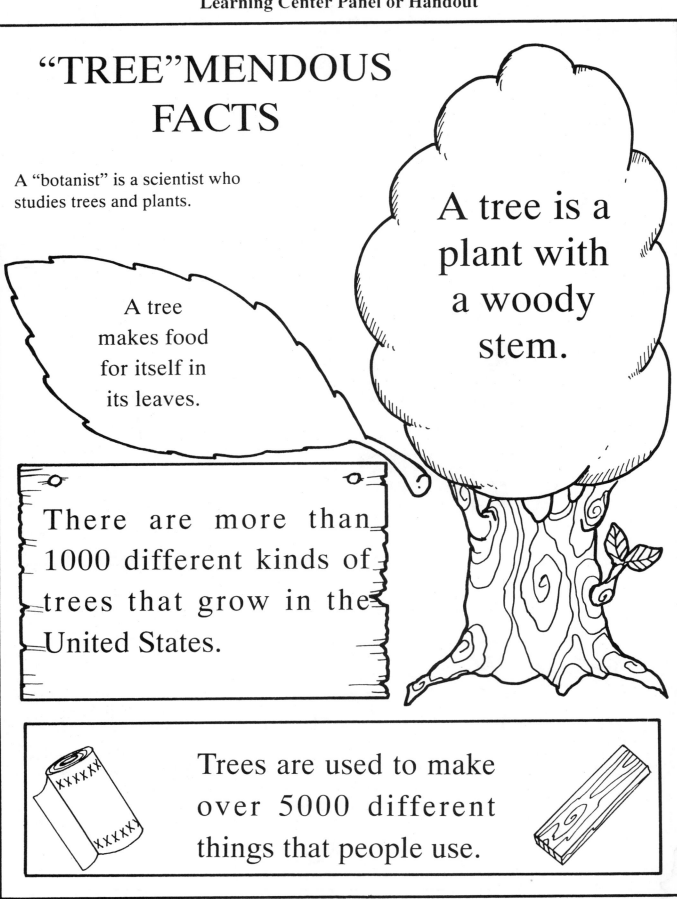

"TREE"MENDOUS FACTS

A "botanist" is a scientist who studies trees and plants.

A tree makes food for itself in its leaves.

A tree is a plant with a woody stem.

There are more than 1000 different kinds of trees that grow in the United States.

Trees are used to make over 5000 different things that people use.

GA1394

SNACK TIME SUGGESTIONS
"Tree"ific Foods

Set a table with samples of foods that grow on trees. If possible include a picture of the tree next to the food, as well as a sample of the whole fruit or nut, with a leaf or stem attached. Some suggestions are

apples	pears
oranges	walnuts
almonds	grapefruit
peaches	cherries
bananas	coconut

Alternate Idea: For younger children, set the table with some foods from trees and some that are not. Let the children try the foods and guess which foods grow on trees. ("Do peanuts grow on trees?") Record their guesses and graph the numbers of "noes" and "yeses." After the guesses, show pictures of where each food comes from.

Note: If you are serving the snack on paper plates or napkins, be sure to tell the children that these are paper products that come from trees, too.

GA1394

GAMES AND SONGS
Forest Penny Toss

Reproduce several copies of the tree pattern below and cut each out. Number each tree, 1, 2, 3... or 5, 10, 15..., depending on the grade level of the children. Tape the numbered trees, close together, to the floor near a wall in your room. Each child takes a turn tossing three pennies against the wall and trying to have the pennies land on a tree. Add up the total points for each child, and the one with the most points wins.

Note: To make the game more interesting, put bonus numbers on the tree trunks and let any child who lands on one have another turn.

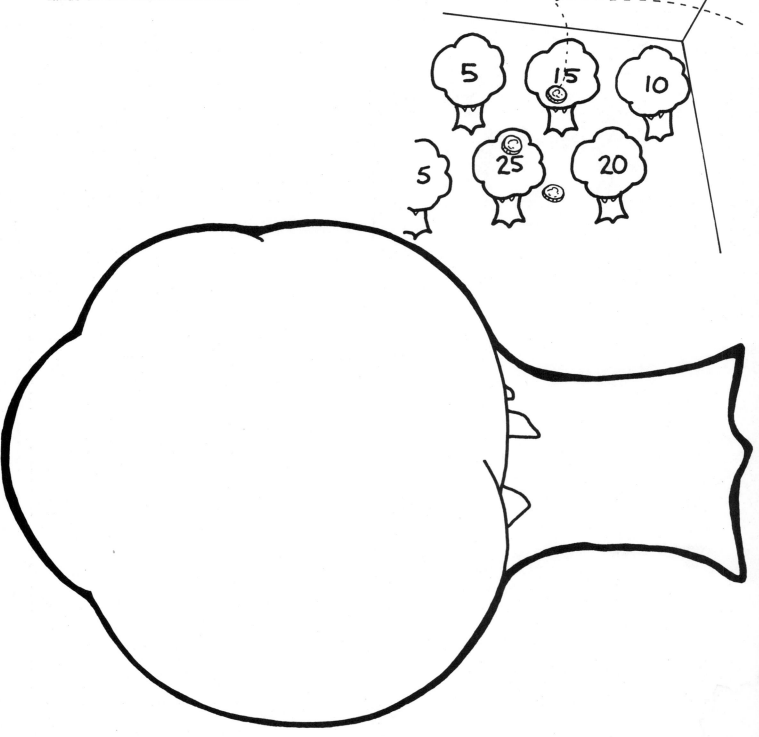

64

GA1394

Draw a circle around all the words that rhyme with *tree*.

65

GA1394

CIRCLE TIME
Thank You, Trees!

Send the note below home, requesting that the children bring a tree product, such as paper or wood, to school to display. Let each child show his/her object and pass it around. Lead a discussion about the variety of things that come from trees and perhaps how some are made. Set a table to display the products. The children can sort the products into categories, such as wood, paper, food or miscellaneous. Have them make posters to hang above the table, featuring more tree products, either drawn or cut from magazines, that are too big for the table: houses, furniture, fences, etc.

Note to Parents

We will be setting up a "tree"mendous display in our room on _____.

"Wood" you please send something that is made from a tree to school for our display? Thanks so much! You're "tree"ific!

GA1394

IMAGINATION PAGE

Imagine you could design your own tree. What would the leaves and branches look like? Would it have any fruit or nuts? Draw a picture of your tree here.

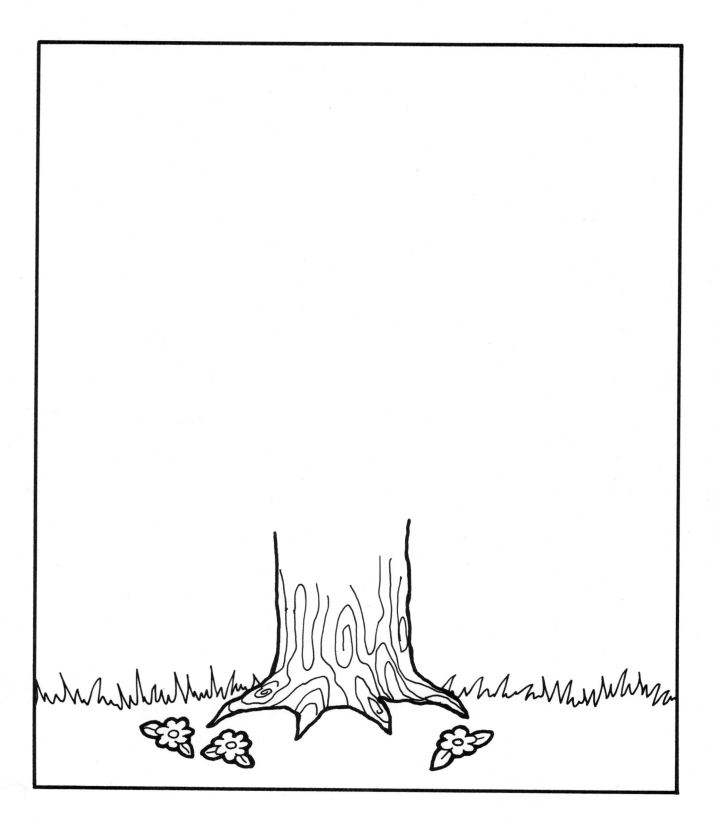

GA1394

CRAFTS
A Classy Tree

For Each Leaf: Put a leaf under a sheet of paper and tape the paper to the table. Using the flat side of an unwrapped crayon, in a fall color, rub the crayon across the paper until the shape of a leaf appears. Cut out the leaf shape.

To Make the Tree: Enlarge the tree trunk pattern to fit the display area. Cut the trunk out of brown paper. Attach the trunk to the wall and tape the leaves to the area above the trunk, overlapping each other to create a beautiful fall tree.

Tree Trunk Pattern

GA1394

Reproduce the note below and send it home with your students to share with their parents.

Dear Parents,
Did you know if everyone recycled his Sunday newspaper, we could save 500,000 trees a week? Here's an idea to make recycling your newspapers easier. Happy recycling!

Find a box that is a little larger than the size of a folded newspaper and about 12" (30.48 cm) deep. Cut a "V"-shaped notch in each side. Lay a piece of heavy string from one notch to the notch on the opposite side. Repeat for the other sides.

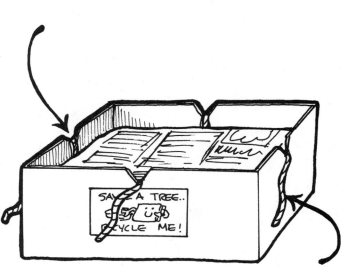

Stack your newspapers on top of the string and tie into a bundle when the box is full.

Here's a family tree for your students to fill out. Reproduce on off-white or tan paper and dab with tea to create an "antique" look.

GA1394

ALL ABOUT APPLES

ACTIVITY
Apple Taste Test

Reproduce the apple pattern below and give one to each child. Cut red, green and yellow apples into wedges. (Dip the wedges into a mixture of water and lemon juice to prevent the apples from turning brown, if you cut them up ahead of time.) Give each child one wedge of each color to taste. Ask children to pick which color apple they thought tasted best and color the apple picture to match it. Tape the colored squares, in lines on a wall, grouped by color. Show the students which color was liked the most and least, by reading the "graph." Make copies of the shape below and cut them out. Ask younger children to describe their favorite apple in one or two words. Write the words in the shape and display the words around your apple graph. Older children can write short poems about the apple and glue the poems to colored construction paper, cut in the shape of an apple. The poems could be written free verse or follow a pattern, such as a haiku or cinquain.

STORY HANDOUT

Cut out and glue this story about apples inside the cover on page 73. Fold in half and read all about apples from winter to fall.

Apple trees can grow anywhere in the world where the summers are warm and sunny and the winters are cold enough to let the trees rest and lose their leaves. Apple growers work all year to be able to harvest the apples in the fall.

In the late winter, the growers cut off old or sick branches on the apple trees. In early spring new trees are planted to replace very old trees. Some trees need to be fed with fertilizer or sprayed to kill pests or stop diseases. When the trees bloom with flowers in the spring, the growers make sure there are lots of bees around to pollinate the flowers. After the flowers fall off, the growers must water the trees during the hot summer days as the apples grow on the branches where the flowers used to be. The apples grow larger and larger until fall, when they are finally picked from the trees by hand or machine. Then the apples are ready for you to eat or to make into apple juice or yummy applesauce!

72

MY APPLE STORY

SNACK TIME SUGGESTIONS
Make Your Own Applesauce
Reproduce the recipe below (laminate if you wish) and display it as you make your own applesauce.

APPLESAUCE

Makes two cups.

6 large, tart apples: peeled and quartered

1/2 cup (120 ml) water

1/2 cup (120 ml) sugar

Bring apples and water to a boil in a heavy pot. Turn to low heat and cover. Simmer 20 minutes, stirring often to prevent sticking. Add more water if the apples seem dry. Press the cooked apples through a sieve into a bowl with a large spoon. Add the sugar, using more or less depending on the tartness of the apples. Add a little cinnamon if you wish. Eat the applesauce warm or chill it in the refrigerator.

GA1394

GAMES AND SONGS
Apple Relay Race

Divide the class into two or four teams, depending on class size. Give each team a tablespoon and a small apple. Line each team up behind a line. While balancing the apple on the spoon, each child takes a turn race-walking (no running!) around a chair, placed at the other end of the room, and back again. He hands the spoon to the next child and the first team to finish wins.

ACTIVITY PAGE
Apple Math Fractions

Draw a line from the apple section to the fraction that matches it.

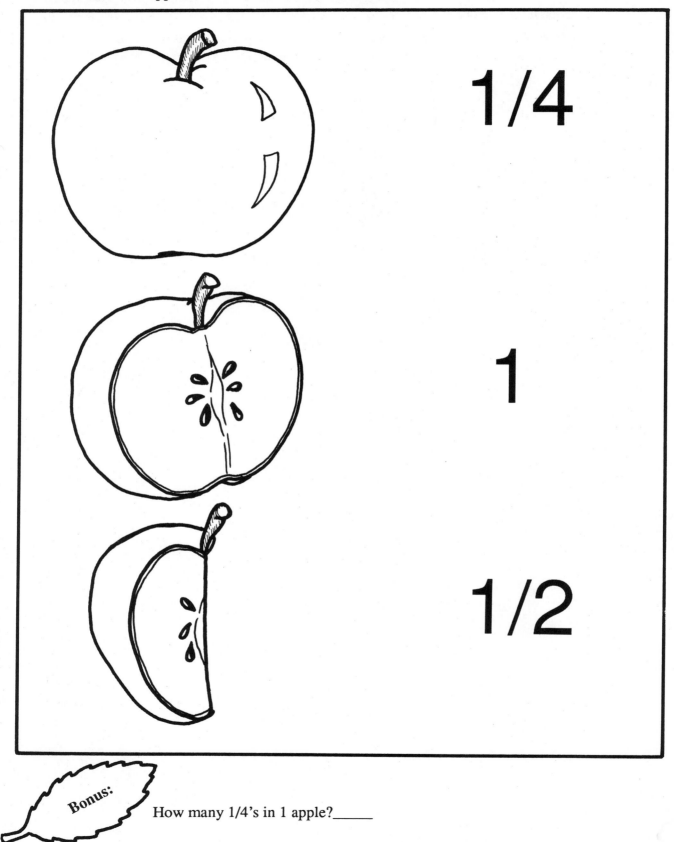

1/4

1

1/2

Bonus: How many 1/4's in 1 apple?_____

GA1394

CIRCLE TIME
Johnny Appleseed

Read the story of Johnny Appleseed to the children. Pass around some apple seeds and a picture of a mature apple tree. Discuss how the tiny seed grows into the large tree. Talk about the "tall tales" found in the story and have the children make up tall tales of their own. Use apples as the subject of the tales and older children can write the story and illustrate it. Younger children can draw the story with a simple caption added, written by an adult. The finished stories can be displayed or put together to create a classroom book of tall apple tales.

Note: A good version of the Johnny Appleseed story is *Johnny Appleseed* by Stephen Kellogg, Scholastic, Inc.

Book Report Paper Topper

Reproduce the topper below on plain or colored paper. Cut out and staple or glue it to the top of lined paper as illustrated. Use as a starter for a book report about Johnny Appleseed.

Johnny Appleseed is a great story because...

IMAGINATION PAGE

Imagine you are an apple, high up in a tree. Pretend to look around and draw a picture of what you see.

CRAFTS
Apple Bookmark

Place the apple pattern below on a piece of folded 4" x 7" (10.16 x 17.78 cm) red construction paper or felt. Cut around the pattern. Repeat for the leaf pattern using a folded piece of 2 1/2" x 6" (6.35 x 15.24 cm) green paper or felt. Open the apple and leaf and carefully spread a thin layer of glue on half of each pattern. (You should use tacky or fabric glue with the felt.) Lay a 9" (22.86 cm) length of 1/4" (.6 cm) dark green or brown ribbon on the pattern as illustrated below. Fold over, carefully matching the edges, and press between layers of wax paper with a heavy weight on top. Let dry.

To Use: Put the apple between the pages in the book and let the ribbon and the leaf hang out.

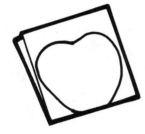

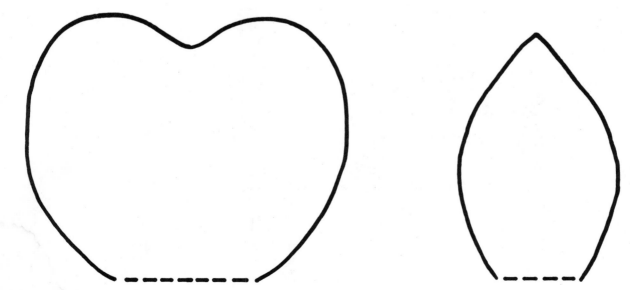

GA1394

TAKE-HOMES
Bendable "Apple Buddies"

Reproduce the pattern below on white or colored heavy paper. Have the students color and cut them out. Punch out the holes with a paper punch. Thread two 12" (6.33 cm) pipe cleaners through the holes, as shown, and bend the ends back about 1/2" (1.25 cm). Tape the pipe cleaners on the back. These also make great room decorations. Reproduce the pattern on "apple"-colored paper (reds, yellows and greens) and use multicolored pipe cleaners.

GA1394

APPLES ARE GOOD FOR ME!

JUICE

APPLESAUCE

GA1394

HOME SWEET HOME

ACTIVITY
Guest Speaker and Display

Invite an architect or building contractor to give a presentation on the basics of home building. They may be able to provide house models or blueprints to illustrate their talk, or examples of the tools that they use every day. Set up a display of pictures of different types of housing (igloos, houseboats, duplexes, etc.) and a table featuring an assortment of building materials, such as small boards, pieces of pipe, wires, etc., for touching and exploring. This would be a great time to bring out all the construction toys and building blocks. Have each child construct a house and display it on a table, marked with masking tape "roads." For an outside activity, mark off a large rectangle in chalk, for each child on the playground. Let the children use chalk to divide their "houses" into "rooms." Connect the houses to each other with chalk "roads" and let them tour each other's houses. You could also number houses and name the streets to provide opportunities for following directions and map reading.

GA1394

BULLETIN BOARD/VISUALS

Directions:

1. Give each child a 5$\frac{1}{2}$" x 8 $\frac{1}{2}$" (13.97 x 21.6 cm) sheet of heavy paper, and have him draw a picture of the outside of his house or apartment (just the building, not the yard).
2. Cut out each house, as close to the outline as possible.
3. Cover a bulletin board with light-green paper. Letter the title across the top of the board.
4. Reproduce the patterns on page 84. Color and cut them out. (You may wish to make several copies, if you have a large board to cover.)
5. Arrange the house cutouts around the board and attach. Use the patterns to decorate the areas between the houses, as shown.
6. Make copies of the sign below and attach to the board, under each house, after the names are added.

PATTERNS

84

GA1394

VISUALS
"Me and My Home" Mini Poster

Reproduce the pattern of the house below. Have each child color it and put his name in the box above the door. Have him cut out the door and window on the heavy lines and paste the house to a piece of white paper, being careful not to get paste on the door or window areas. Cut out the house on the heavy outline. Each child is to draw a picture of himself behind the door and a picture of a favorite object in his home behind the window shutters.

GA1394

Pretzel Building Sticks

Give each child a handful of small pretzel sticks and let him make house shapes. The pretzels can be broken to create different lengths of sticks to work with.

Cheese 'n' Cracker House

Top a square cracker, such as a saltine, with a triangle cut from a slice of processed cheese. Add a broccoli "tree" or two.

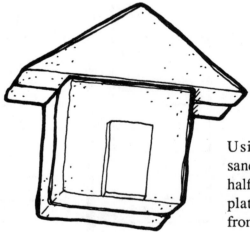

House Sandwiches

Using your favorite sandwiches, cut half of the sandwiches into fourths, on the diagonal. Cut the other half into squares. Position two sandwich sections on each plate, as shown, to resemble a house. Add a door, cut from cheese or lunch meat, if you wish.

GA1394

GAMES AND SONGS
All Around the House Obstacle Course

String colorful yarn from a starting point, around the classroom or playground to create an obstacle course. At each obstacle label the instructions for completing it. For example, string the yarn to a table and around the leg and underneath it. Attach signs as illustrated. Have each child follow the yarn through the course. For larger classrooms, you may create different courses using several colors of yarn to mark each course. If you like, you may also label each obstacle with the name of a room in a house as well as the instructions for completing it.

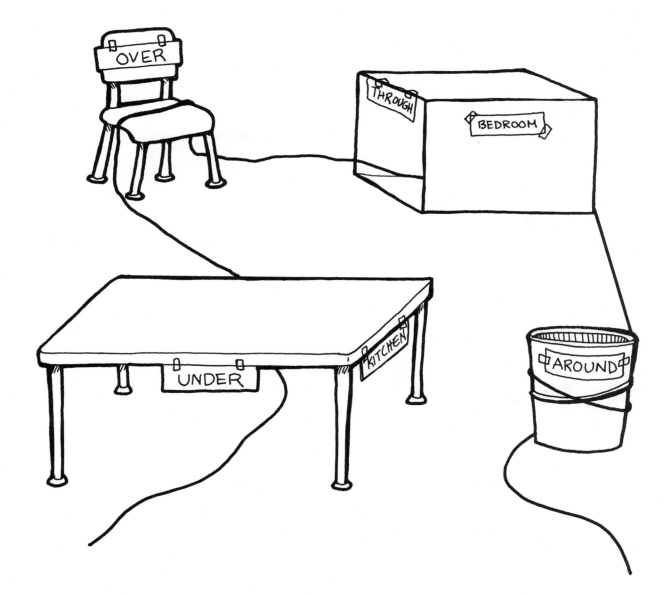

GA1394

ACTIVITY PAGE
Scrambled House
Unscramble the words below to discover objects in a house. Use the pictures as clues to help you.

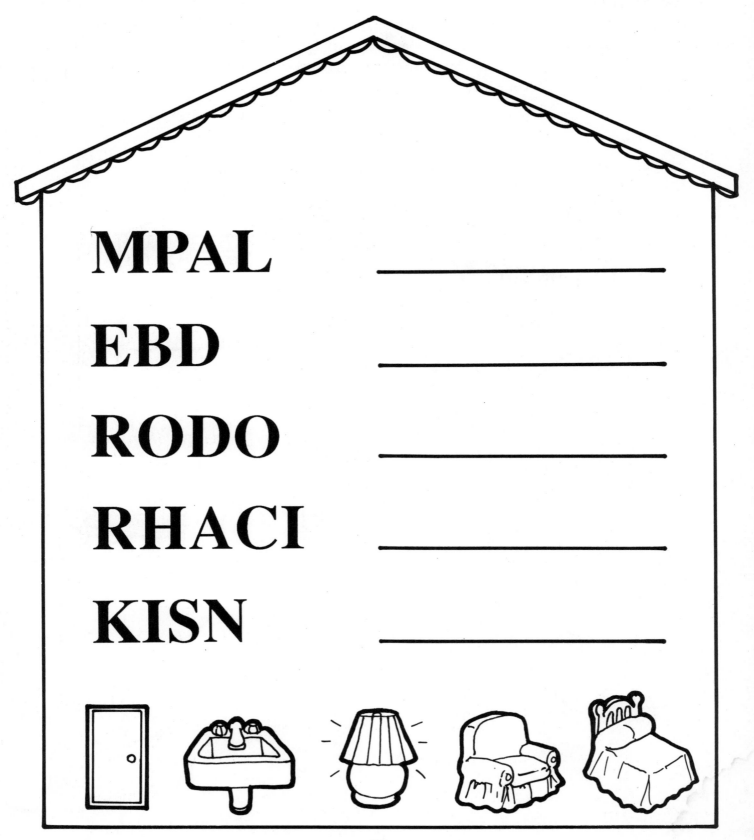

MPAL _____

EBD _____

RODO _____

RHACI _____

KISN _____

GA1394

CIRCLE TIME
Animals Need Homes, Too!

Lead a discussion on animals and their homes. Talk about the uses animals have for their homes, from storing food to hiding from their enemies. Give the different names for animal homes, such as den, burrow, nest, etc., and show examples, if possible. Pass around a snail's shell or bird's nest. Ask children about their pets and where they sleep. Do they have dog or cat houses? Make copies of the animals and their houses matching cards below. Cut apart and laminate if you wish. Let the children try to make matching pairs of animals and their houses.

GA1394

IMAGINATION PAGE

Imagine that you could add a new room to your house or apartment. What would it be used for? What would you put in it? Draw a picture of it below.

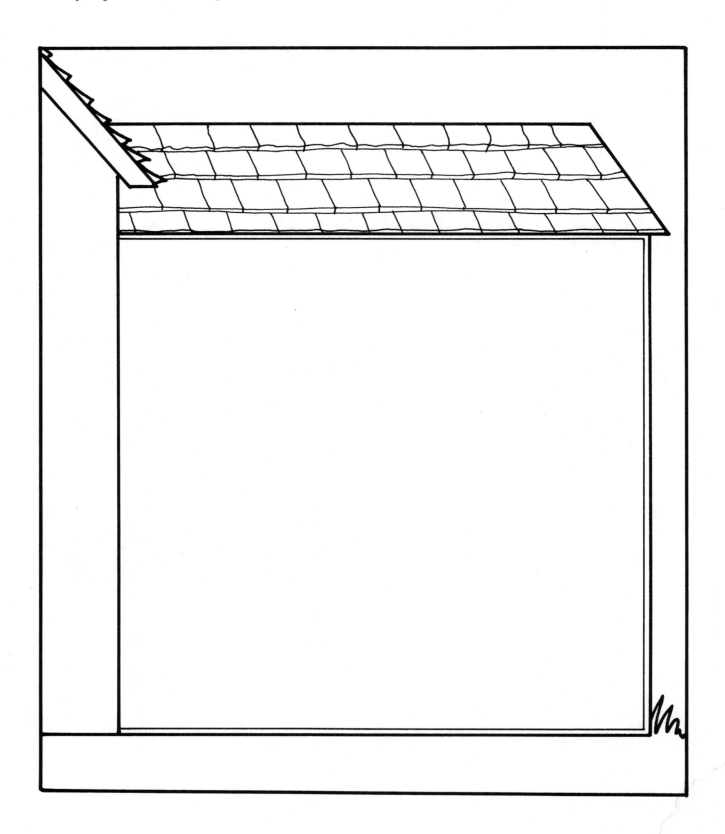

CRAFTS
Home Sweet Home Wind Chimes

Using a colorful plastic drinking cup, punch several holes around the rim with a paper punch. Make a small hole in the top and tie a piece of string through the hole for a hanger, as shown below. Tie different lengths of string through the other holes and attach metal objects, such as keys, bells and buttons to the strings. Make sure some of the objects are tied at about the same length, so they will hit each other. Decorate the cup with stickers and hang in a breezy protected spot to make beautiful music.

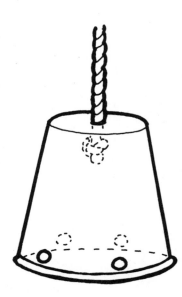

91

Reproduce the book patterns below on white or light-colored paper. Cut out and staple or glue the edges together to form a book. Have each child fill in the information after he has memorized the numbers.

My phone number is

My address is

My emergency phone number is

Staple or glue cover here

I KNOW MY "HOME" NUMBERS

Name

GA1394

EXTRAS
Home Sweet Home Door Hanger

Reproduce the pattern below on heavy white or colored paper. Cut out and color if desired. Fill in the child's name and send these hangers home with the children to decorate their doors.

_____'S

Cut out.

Home Sweet Home

GA1394

MAKE A MONSTER

ACTIVITY
Monster Exhibit and Dress Up Day

Ask each child to come to school dressed as a silly or scary monster (no masks). Reproduce the eyes, mouths and noses on the following pages. Cut them apart and place the parts in labeled bags or boxes, as shown. Have each child pick one paper from each bag and glue his monster face on a paper plate. Color the face, if you wish, and add hair made from yarn bits, Easter grass or shredded colored paper. Each child's creation will be unique. Display the faces or add bodies made from tracing the children's bodies on large sheets of paper. Draw on any details and clothing, and attach to the paper plate face, as illustrated below. Hang on the walls, along with any monster posters or drawings. Invite other classes to visit your "Monster Museum."

94

GA1394

PATTERNS

Eyes: (Cut pairs apart after selection.)

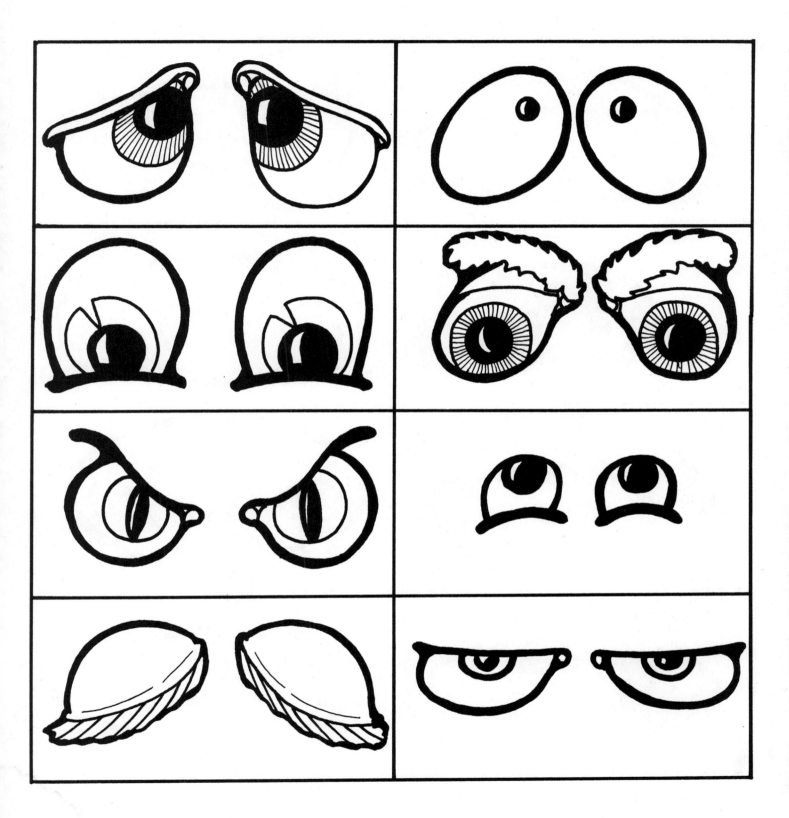

PATTERNS

Noses: You can use these for the Pin the Nose on the Monster game on page 99.

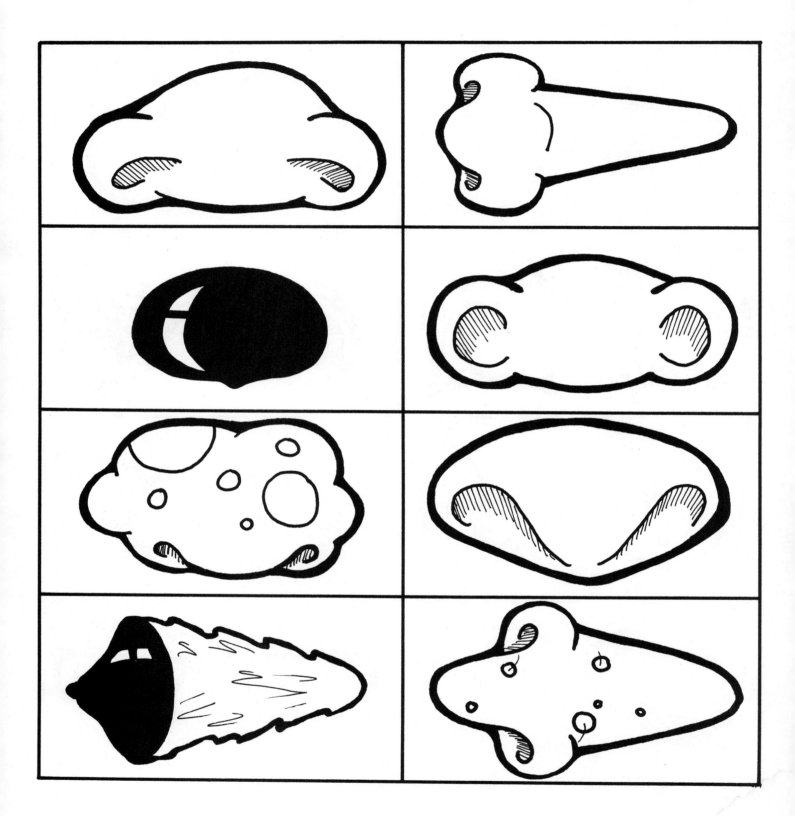

96

PATTERNS

Mouths: These can be turned upside down, too.

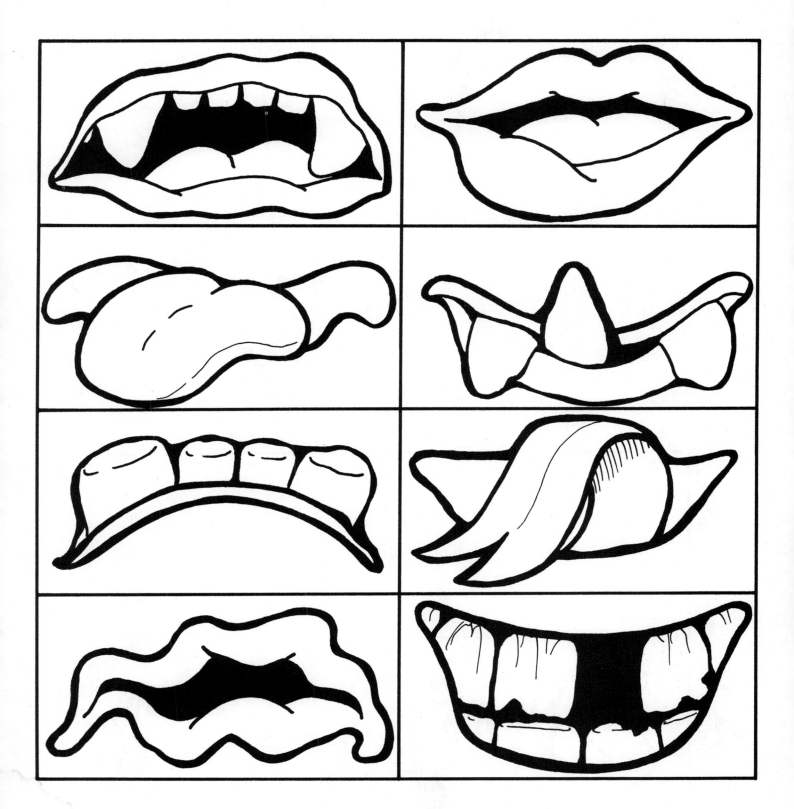

SNACK TIME SUGGESTIONS
My Monster Mix

Give your students their own packages of personalized snack mix. Mix snack ingredients from the list below, adding your own ideas. Put the snack mixture in small sandwich bags. Fold copies of the label below and staple onto the tops of the sandwich bags, as shown. Decorate the back of the label with stickers or markers. (Personalize the label with your name before copying or your student's name afterward.)

Monster Mix Ingredients

Gummi Worms or Spiders
raisins
candy corn
toasted pumpkin seeds
miniature marshmallows
chocolate or peanut butter chips

animal crackers
blue corn chips
miniature pretzels
dinosaur-shaped cookies
assorted cereals
dried fruit bits

GAMES AND SONGS
Pin the Nose on the Monster!

Reproduce this page and the noses on page 96. Cut out the monster head and attach to a wall. Cut out the noses and put a piece of rolled masking tape or double-sided tape on the back of each. Each child takes a turn, blindfolded, trying to place the nose on the monster's face. The child who comes closest wins. Be sure to play some "spooky" music, to set the mood. "The Monster Mash" or a Halloween sound effects record would make great background music.

GA1394

ACTIVITY PAGE
Space Monster Pattern Match

Cut out the squares below and paste them on the space monster, matching the patterns. Color the picture.

GA1394

CIRCLE TIME
What Monsters Are Afraid Of

Reproduce the finger puppet and note card below. Cut them out and tape the ends of the finger puppet base together, so it will fit on a child's finger. Give one puppet to each child and lead a discussion about common childhood fears. Talk about the differences between "real" and "pretend" and about makeup and special effects on TV and in the movies. Ask each child what he thinks his monster might be afraid of. Write their answers on the note cards along with suggestions that their monsters might use to cope with their fears. Maybe they could talk to their Mommy or Daddy monsters or turn on night-lights. Explore ways the children could deal with any fears they may have. Make a booklet from the note cards, by punching two holes in the left edge and binding them together with colorful yarn. Make a cover of heavy paper decorated with a cutout of the finger puppet, if you wish.

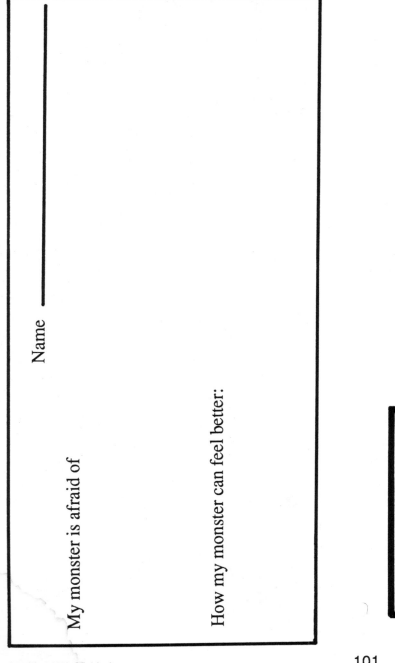

Name

My monster is afraid of

How my monster can feel better:

My Monster is afraid!

GA1394

IMAGINATION PAGE

Imagine you are eating lunch with your friend, a monster. What did his mommy put in his lunch box? Draw it below.

GA1394

CRAFTS
Monster from Space Paper Bag Puppet

Reproduce the pattern below. Cut out and attach to bottom of a folded lunch bag. Punch out the holes and insert a pipe cleaner into each. Twist together, as shown, and glue or tape the circles on the ends.

Extra Ideas: Use colored or metallic-looking paper bags and decorate the face and antennae with silver glitter. Use a glue stick to "dot" the bag and sprinkle with the glitter to create a spotted "body."

Reproduce the sign below on plain or colored, heavy paper. Have each child color and cut out the sign, and punch out the holes, using a paper punch. Attach a piece of colorful yarn as a hanger. Send these home for the children to put in their rooms.

GA1394

EXTRAS
Monster Shape Book

Use this monster to make a cover for theme stories or attach it to the front of a folder. This can also be used as a Halloween card. Just reduce it to the size you like and make copies.

GA1394

TAKE A TRIP

ACTIVITY
Around the World Tour

Following the instructions on page 107, create several "foreign country" centers at different tables in your classroom. Divide your class into "tour groups," one for each center. Assign each group a "destination" and have them "travel" to that country to visit and complete any activities. Give the groups an appropriate amount of time to "tour" their countries and then switch centers until each group has visited each center.

Note: Children can complete the "Take-a-Trip Suitcase" (page 115) and follow with the "Postcard" (page 117) when they have finished their "trips."

Travel Ticket

Reproduce the ticket below on heavy paper. Cut out and fill in the information. At each center the children can have their tickets stamped or punched with a paper punch.

TICKET

DATE

PUNCH HERE

FOR: _____

TO: _____

Pattern

INSTRUCTIONS
How to Make a Foreign Country Center

1. Fold a piece of 11" x 17" (27.94 x 43.18 cm) cardboard in half, lengthwise and tape it in the shape of a tent, to the center of a table.

2. Make copies of the Table Topper information sheet on page 108. Fill in the information for the country you will be "touring" on page 108 and outline or highlight the location of the country on the map on page 109. Tape or glue each sheet to one side of the cardboard, as illustrated.

3. Surround the Table Topper display with pictures and objects that would further illustrate the country, such as travel brochures, currency, native crafts or foods.

4. Prepare an activity or two to complete at the center. Some suggestions: Fill out a questionnaire about the information found at the center, pick a favorite object and draw a picture of it, complete a native craft (origami, for example), learn a foreign word or two, sample a new food.

GA1394

GA1394

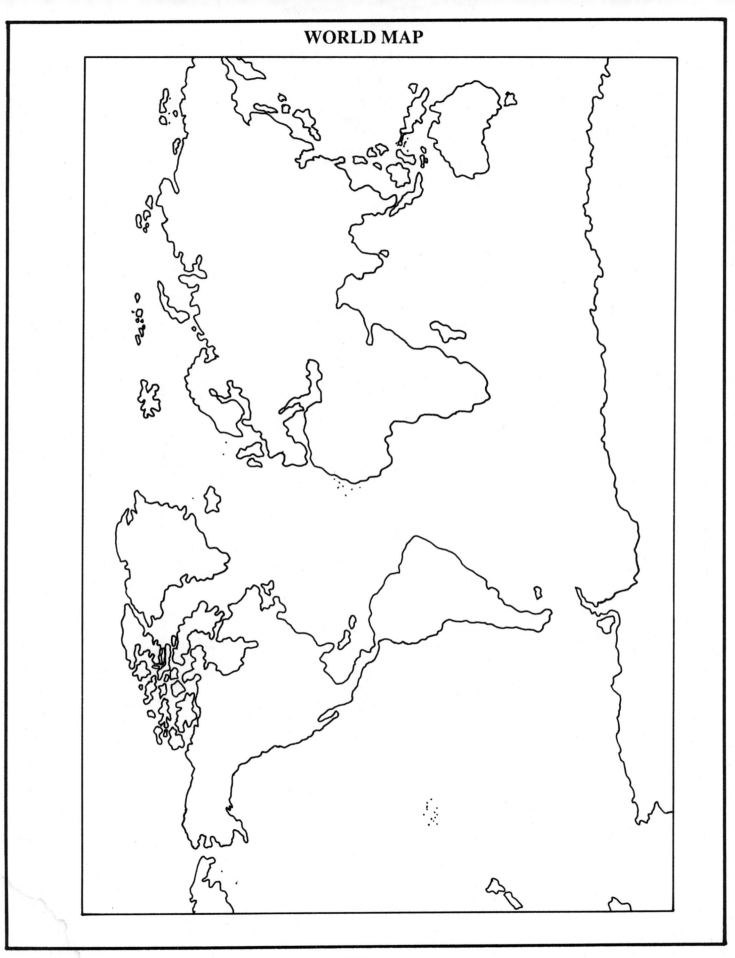

GA1394

SNACK TIME SUGGESTIONS
Foods Around the World

Using a classroom world map (or enlarge the map on page 109) as a background, set up a table with samples of foods from other countries arranged on top. Attach a colorful piece of yarn to the country on the map and string it to the native food below. Tape it to the table behind the food. Repeat with the other foods. Encourage the children to try any new and unusual foods. Foods to try include nachos, fortune cookies, buttered rice, spaghetti, chop suey, pierogi, German sausages and crepes.

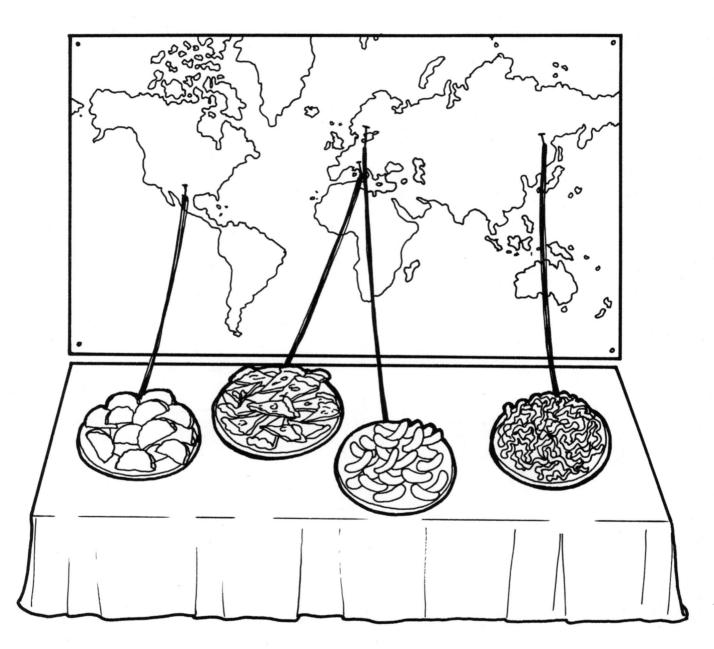

GA1394

GAMES AND SONGS
Transportation Mime

While playing lively music, such as "It's a Small World After All," call out the names of different forms of transportation and have the children act them out to the song. Some transportation suggestions are listed below.

airplanes
cable cars
submarines
hot air balloons
bicycles
motorboats
your own car
school bus
space shuttle
skateboards
motorcycles
roller skates

GA1394

ACTIVITY PAGE
The Right Path

Match these pictures to the map below to see what path to take. Trace the correct path with your pencil or crayon.

Start → (tree) → (fence) → MAIL → **Finish**

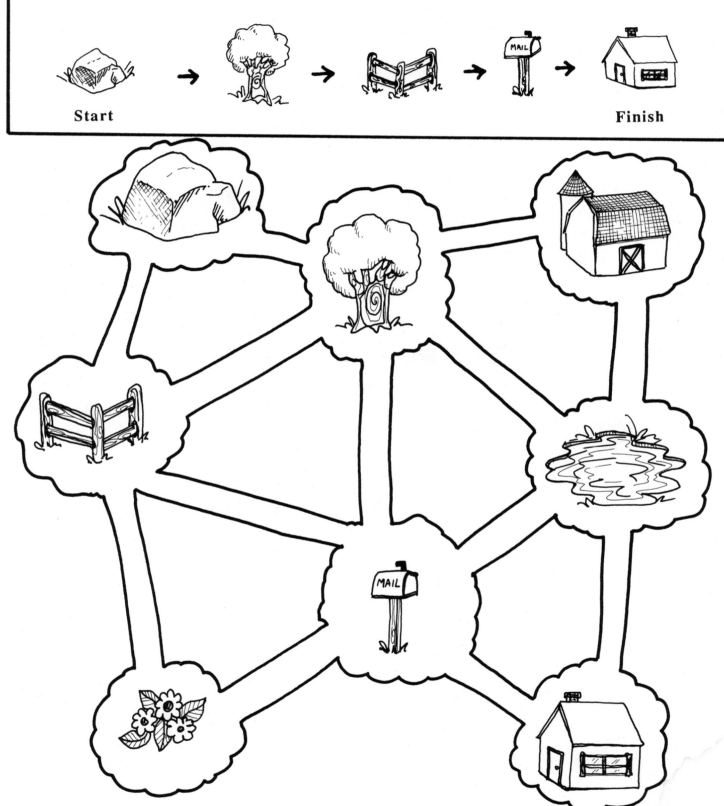

112

CIRCLE TIME
A Visit to Our Hometown

Prepare a presentation of the special attractions and points of interest that make your town or city someplace people would like to visit. Be sure to mention any historical events, as well as any famous landmarks or scenic areas. Pass around photos or postcards, and find out if anyone has visited the places pictured. Let the children give you the reasons why they think your town is special. After the discussion, have the children draw travel posters to illustrate the reasons. Display them at school or even city hall!

GA1394

IMAGINATION PAGE

Imagine you are the pilot of a hot air balloon that lands in a place you've never visited. Draw a picture of what you see when you land.

GA1394

CRAFTS
Take- a-Trip Suitcase

Lay a copy of the pattern below on top of an unfolded paper lunch bag. Trace the handle area, as illustrated below, and cut it out. (Cut through all layers of paper bag.) Label the bag and decorate it, if desired. Open the bag and fold down or cut off the tabs on the sides of the bag. This project can be done before the other "Take a Trip" activities and used to carry passports, tickets and other items.

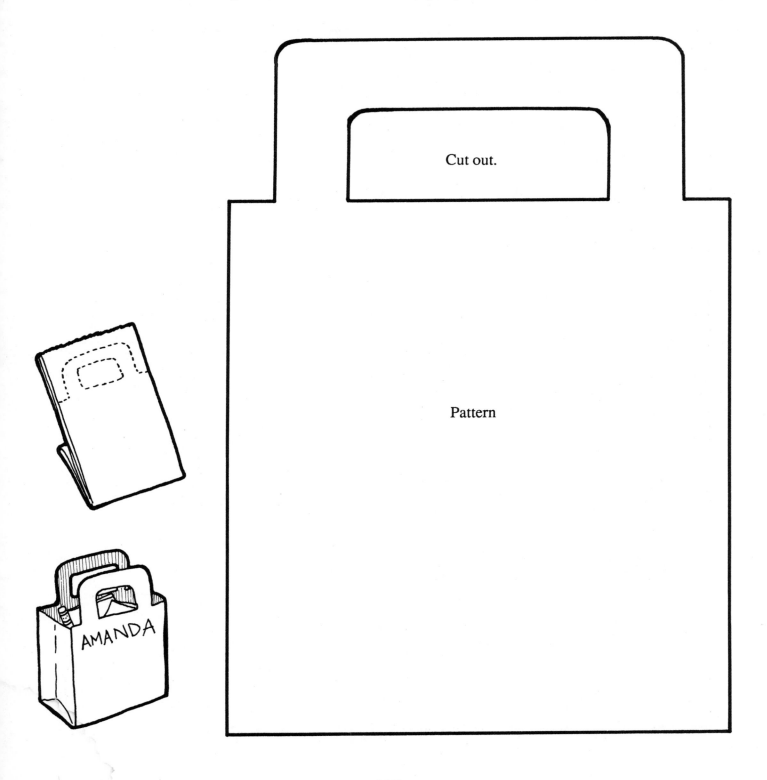

Cut out.

Pattern

GA1394

Reproduce the passport below. Fold in half lengthwise and in half again to form a booklet. Have each child fill in the information and carry it with him on his "trip."

(country)

(state)   (city)

(street)

My address is _____

(color)

My hair is _____

(color)

My eyes are _____

This is me.

Places I've Visited

PASSPORT

Name

GA1394

EXTRAS
Postcard

Reproduce the postcard below. Cut out on the solid line and fold in half on the dotted line. Glue or tape the card shut. Draw a picture in the box on the front of a place you've "visited." Write a message and address on the back.

To:

GA1394

THEME CLIP ART

Use these clip art characters to decorate newsletters, awards, announcements, certificates, etc. They can also be used to create theme-related bookmarks and stickers.

SMART COOKIES

UNDER THE SEA

TEDDY BEAR BUDDIES

WEATHER WATCHERS

TERRIFIC TEETH

"TREE"MENDOUS TREES

ALL ABOUT APPLES

HOME SWEET HOME

MAKE A MONSTER

TAKE A TRIP

GA1394

Name_____

Paste clip art here before copying.

Our class is planning a special day and we need some help.

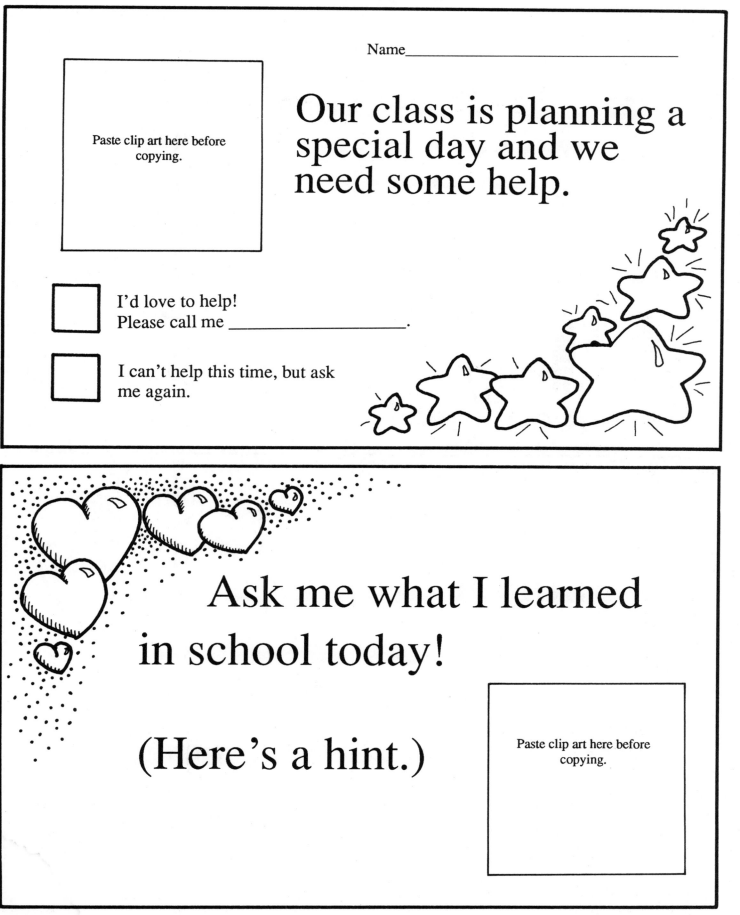

☐ I'd love to help!
Please call me _____.

☐ I can't help this time, but ask me again.

Ask me what I learned in school today!

(Here's a hint.)

Paste clip art here before copying.

GA1394

was all
ears today!

was a
"dino-mite"
kid today!

IS A
SUPER

STAR!

DID AN
"OUTSTANDING"
JOB TODAY!

GA1394